FINAL
DEPARTURES

Also by Barry Albin Dyer

Don't Drop the Coffin!

FINAL DEPARTURES

AROUND THE WORLD WITH BRITAIN'S
MOST REMARKABLE UNDERTAKER

BARRY ALBIN DYER

Hodder & Stoughton

LONDON SYDNEY AUCKLAND

Copyright © 2003 by Barry Albin Dyer

First published in Great Britain in 2003

The right of Barry Albin Dyer to be identified as the Author of
the Work has been asserted by him in accordance with
the Copyright, Designs and Patents Act 1988.

10 9 8 7 6 5 4 3 2

British Library Cataloguing in Publication Data
A record for this book is available from the British Library

ISBN 0 340 86163 0

Typeset in Goudy by Avon DataSet Ltd,
Bidford-on-Avon, Warwickshire

Printed and bound in Great Britain by
Clays Ltd, St Ives plc

The paper and board used in this paperback are natural
recyclable products made from wood grown in sustainable forests.
The manufacturing processes conform to the environmental
regulations of the country of origin.

Hodder & Stoughton
A Division of Hodder Headline Ltd
338 Euston Road
London NW1 3BH
www.madaboutbooks.com

To all those who have made a difference to my life, many of whom have gone from this world but not from inside me.

To my sons Simon and Jonathan and my grandchildren – always remember that *you are the future*.

Things change, life ends, but love goes on.

Contents

Acknowledgements

To the countless funeral journals from around the world for their inspiration, articles and information: *The Funeral Director, The Funeral Journal, Pharos, Thanos,* FIAT/IFTA, *The American Funeral Director Journal* (BIFD), *Funerals of the Famous, The Funeral Times, The Immortalist.*

David Pascal, Bob Ettinger and staff at the Cryonics Institute, Chicago, US.

Death: A Users Guide for some interesting points.

Carole Bearden for her support and encouragement throughout the past 15 years.

Newspapers and magazines and many wonderful journalists for their worldwide tales.

The endless dedication of all those involved with the death care industry.

My sons Simon and Jonathan, my Dad, my partner Jackie, friends, staff and family: bless you. All my love and sincere thanks always.

Paul Darnell for his eagle eye and support.

Alan Ball and the action and production team of *Six Feet Under* for your wonderful inspiration, and the actors, writers and production team of the brilliant *Sins*, with a special thanks to Frank Finlay for his portrayal of Uncle Irwin.

Greg Watts, who taught me how to write, but only half as well as he does.

My friend Peter Hindley: thank you.

My friend Gino (Janny): ciao, ciao bambino.

Joanna, Jackie and Jan Fletcher for hours of dedication and help.

The wonderful people of Bermondsey, Rotherhithe and South London.

Father Andre Ravier for *The Body of St Bernadette*.

Special thanks to The National Association of Funeral Directors.

A sincere thank you for Jan for two great sons – they are a credit to us both.

Everyone I know and those I don't but know me!

Thanks.

Introduction

Dear Barry . . .

. . . I miss my granddad terribly but your book alleviated many of the nightmares I had concerning his passing. Your book made me look at death in a different way . . .

Nothing could have prepared me for the overwhelming response to my first book, *Don't Drop the Coffin!* I knew that the book – a memoir of my upbringing within F. A. Albin & Sons, one of the UK's oldest family firms of funeral directors, my subsequent accession to ownership of this grand old company and an honest account of the vast diversity of tasks an undertaker faces as part of his daily routine – was, shall we say, unique. As my publisher warned me, there had not previously been a great demand for books about the funeral industry – this one had the potential either to become a cult hit or sink into obscurity! However, I knew I had a story that needed to be told. Not just for me, but for the sake of a profession that is grossly misrepresented and misunderstood; for the sake of my wonderful, devoted staff whose work provides such comfort to thousands of people every year yet goes unheralded; for the funeral directors around the country and around the world who are popularly portrayed as dour and unsmiling as the Grim Reaper himself; and for the countless bereaved families and friends that we have had the privilege of serving. Every one of these people has a story deserving of a book in itself, but few of them have the means to make it widely known. If my book could bring comfort, under-standing or recognition to just a handful of these people, I would have been satisfied with a job well done.

But the letters kept arriving! I have been deeply moved by the incredible generosity of the comments of so many readers, and privileged that so many were moved to open their hearts and tell me some deeply personal stories with which my book seems to have helped them come to terms. One man kindly emailed: 'I have enjoyed every page and it has made sense of my desire to come into the funeral business. I have wanted to for many years but because it wasn't on any careers guidance course I attended in my youth, I felt I must be a little strange. I have realised now that it's a calling that goes hand in hand with my desire to help people, and the perfectionist in me.' For one woman, *Don't Drop the Coffin!* inspired her to write for some advice on matters of the heart: 'I felt compelled to write to you and congratulate you on your marvellous book. I laughed, cried and couldn't put it down. My boyfriend is in your trade. I empathised with you when you said you have to have a certain amount of emotional detachment, but X is so laid-back he's almost in the coffin! He's a lovely guy and

I love him to bits, but he doesn't show his emotional side very often. Is it a hazard of the job? Am I ever to wonder what makes him tick?' I am probably not best qualified to answer all the questions this young lady raised, but I was touched that my book struck a chord and that she felt able to write to me in this way.

The book has led me into contact with so many wonderful people, and led me down paths that I would never have dreamed. Most notably, it has inspired an ITV television series of the same name. For several months my staff and I have been filmed in all aspects of our work by Ginger Television. It has been an experience like no other and the crew became part of the Albins family for the duration of their time with us. I have described this at length in the Introduction to a new edition of the book which was published to coincide with the programme's broadcast.

It was some months ago, while reflecting on the many changes to the life of Albins that the book has set in motion and, if I'm honest, feeling a little empty from no longer having a personal project to occupy my time, that I turned to an old and trusted friend. 'My Albin Stamp Album' is a book I keep in my office, containing every stamp I have ever received from abroad. I find it a wonderful and inspiring *aide-mémoire*, turning the pages to remind me of the course of my business life to date and of the start of some wonderful friendships. I have always believed that the mind is a kind of photo album. Each page we turn is a memory revisited – sometimes joyful, sometimes painful but always true and meaningful.

There was a knock at the door and there was Jackie with my first cup of tea of the day. Seeing me in deep thought she quietly placed the tea on the corner of the desk and, without a word, diplomatically retreated.

The first stamp on the page was from the USA, and took me back to those exciting days of my first visits to that wonderful country. As I cast my eyes across the page the stamps became pictures, not of the famous people they depicted but of old friends, good times and bad times, times I had made money and times I had lost it. A stamp portraying the First Lady of America became that of my best friend in America, Carole, and the first baseball game she had taken me to. I remembered our visit to the Rosewood Funeral Home in Houston, a place that affected my future so much. Then, in stark contrast, I came across a stamp from Iran depicting the wonderful history of Persia (as it was once known). The face of my old friend Samazadeh drifted into my thoughts, with his wonderful kind smile and a pocket always full of pistachio nuts.

Reaching for my tea, still engrossed in my thoughts, I accidentally knocked the cup from my desk to the floor. The cup bounced and hit the floor for a second time, breaking into eight distinct pieces. Within moments, the tea had spread everywhere, over the floor and on to my feet, bringing me sharply back into the world of the present!

As I looked at the eight pieces of china it came to my mind that while the cup was no longer a cup - it could no longer be used for the purpose for which it was made - the tea was still tea. A mess, to be sure, but still tea. I thought to myself that that is exactly what happens to us when we die: our bodies break and can no longer be used for their purpose, but our true selves - our spirits, souls or love, whatever word we use to describe the truly unknown - are no longer contained in one place. Instead we spread out, no longer restricted by physical containment, and in some way we go on, too free to be brought to an end, unlike the cup!

It was then, with the colours and cultures of so many nations displayed on the pages of the stamp album in front of me, that I realised there was still so much more to be told. Italy, Malaysia, Spain, Jersey, Eire, Zimbabwe, Lourdes, Australia, Greece, Guernsey, Iran, USA, Jamaica . . . and these just on the first few pages. Death is a wonderful mystery that affects every single one of us, not only those who have passed through the doors of our humble business here in south-east London. I felt privileged to have had such an insight and contact with cultures around the globe, and I decided at that moment that my next task was to try and record in a new book all the knowledge and wisdom I had picked up on my travels and encounters in the strange, stigmatised world of funerals, death and bereavement.

Final Departures is intended as more than another memoir. The stories herein go wider than my own travel journal. Not just geographically, to Europe, the States and the Far East, but through time as well. The embalming techniques perfected by the Ancient Egyptians still demand detailed study by today's professionals, and there are pointers to rituals of the future also, such as the steadily expanding industry of cryonics and the slightly less common option of having one's ashes blasted into space. This is no academic tome, no definitive historical volume. But I have written it to entertain and enlighten, perhaps as much as anything to deepen my own understanding of the wonderful mystery of death, which comes to us all whatever our customs. Please fasten your seatbelts and enjoy the journey!

1

Embalmondsey

Whatever your chosen method of final departure, this is one of the – if not *the* – most important days of your life, when for a moment you become the centre of everything. For those left behind, and for the funeral director employed, this is, quite literally, a grave responsibility!

As a child of the 1960s, I grew up in the heady days of the cold war and the threat of impending catastrophe, with Nikita Khrushchev as Russian leader. When Khrushchev was removed from office by the very people who had placed him there, he passed two confidential, sealed letters to his successor. On one envelope, he wrote, 'The first time something goes seriously wrong, open this letter'; on the second, he put, 'The second time something goes seriously wrong, open this letter'. For a long while, all went well for the new Russian Premier, but then a huge international crisis landed on his desk. In desperation, he opened the first letter, which simply read 'Blame me'. This, it is said, he did, and he scraped through by the skin of his teeth. A year later, he faced yet another problem, this time within his own country, so he turned to the second letter. This, when opened, read 'Write two letters . . .' So, you see, when you are dealing with other people's emotions or are responsible for any service that cannot have a dress rehearsal, you must not fail. To me, all funerals are that important.

Bereavement is, I have always believed, responsible for a huge percentage of mental illness. Don't ever underestimate the true importance of a funeral - it is the first step we all take to recovery after a loved one has died. Bereavement can cause so many ailments, not just mental but physical too, and although we deal with this pain in many different ways, deal with it we must. During the trip round the world that we will take in this book, the power of bereavement must never be forgotten. The 'departure lounge' for this trip will be my own area of London - Bermondsey - and the wonderful people who live here.

Take Albert, for example, a lovely old man who had lost his wife. Married for 40 years without any children, he stood at the grave with five other mourners - Father Michael Cooley, a Priest from Melior Street Church, Bermondsey, the conductor, the grave-digger and Albert's two sisters, Lil and Elsie. As Father Michael gave the final blessing, the two ladies said, 'Albert, we can't see our flowers.' The Priest replied, 'Perhaps they're the two Oases on the coffin along with Albert's', at which point this charming old man jumped a metre down into the grave and onto the coffin lid. All those present gasped with horror, worried for his safety and of course a little shocked by his actions. Standing on the top of the coffin, Albert bent down and then popped up with the cards - ' 'Ere Lil, this is yours, and that's yours, Elsie' – before scrambling back to the edge of the grave as if nothing had happened. Disrespectful? Not at all! Albert had just, without considering his actions, followed his instincts and was dealing with his loss by taking part, however unorthodox it might have seemed.

Another man, diving into his brother's grave, was caught by the ankles and, struggling in desperation, had to be prised from the depths of the grave by six strong men. This man had abandoned hope and all logical thinking. He was only inches away from serious injury, but no physical injury could have compared with the emotional injury inflicted by the loss of his brother. Believe it or not, this man's road to recovery began with that leap. This path to recovery may be hard and long as we learn not to get over the loss but to live with it, taking a new step every day – sometimes forwards, sometimes backwards – but nevertheless a new step each day.

The American term for people who throw themselves at or into a coffin is 'casket climbers'. Years of experience help you to predict when this might happen, body language and eye movements giving the greatest clues. There are several different kinds of climber, but all are genuine. They may be desperate to show their grief or have a true need to be with the one they love so much but can no longer touch in the same way. There may be disbelief that the death has occurred, a numbness, but, as with the man above, this final leap will often prove very important in coming to terms with the death itself. We never try to stop the intention completely, just to protect both the deceased and the mourner. The best funeral directors, like the best football referees, are not noticed until they are needed.

Some people find every reason possible to put off this final departure. A colleague of mine had a four-year responsibility to a lady who had died leaving two feuding daughters – one wishing to have Mum cremated, the other wishing to have her buried. I am told that the sisters took injunctions out to prevent each other doing anything, so Mum was going nowhere. None of the authorities would take responsibility, and it was left to the 'fourth emergency service', the undertaker, to patiently handle what was happening. As far as I know, this extraordinary situation still exists. The sisters still do not talk to each other and on alternate days they visit the coffin, containing the hermetically sealed, embalmed remains of their mum, still not laid to rest. The flowers they bring are put on the coffin only on the days they visit, and the two sisters check to make sure that only their own flowers are there.

These two ladies are in truth refusing to let go. All the time they are in dispute, they are still holding on. If they could step back and look clearly at the reasons they are giving for not laying their mum to rest, they would have to face up to the fact that, either way, their mum is still dead, and they appear to be in denial. Without facing up to this, the outcome could be gloomy – eventually they will no longer have their mum to visit, and, because of their anger, they will have lost each other too.

But not all departures take this long to achieve. In my last book, *Don't Drop the Coffin!*, I described the funeral of Big Arthur, the breakdown truck man, at which the hearse broke down and my friend Paul towed it with his own black Rolls-Royce. Ironic, isn't it? – Big Arthur breaking down at his own funeral and being towed the rest of the way to make sure he got there on time! His lovely family thought it very fitting indeed.

Paul, a tough but very kind character, runs a security firm looking after VIPs for the government and large companies. When a dear friend of his recently died, Paul decided that his friend would be king of the road for a day and nothing would stop our journey or hold us up. Paul placed cars with lights and sirens at every junction and himself led the funeral cortège, a hearse and 12 limousines. Every male member of the family wore a morning suit with gold waistcoat, and even Paul's staff had the same matching clothes. The casket was a beautiful Batesville Premier, and Paul's friend was laid to rest at home near Biggin Hill in Kent.

We sedately walked the funeral for the first half-mile from the house before Paul's escort machine swung into action with burly men at each set of lights, stopping the traffic and then zooming past the cortège to the next junction. We were instructed to keep up, but I made it clear that I was not prepared to break the pace that was appropriate. Although such slow progress to the cemetery was once a purely practical requirement so that the mourners' candles would not be blown out, it is now a mark of respect. Although Paul understood, he was still determined that we would not stop until we reached the cemetery, moving on like some royal convoy with the whole world stopping for us. This was Paul's way of coping, the only way he knew how, with the loss.

As we entered the slip road to the cemetery, Paul, desperate to get back in front of us for the final entry to the gates, clipped the front wing of the hearse. After the beautiful service, full of well-chosen music and words, Paul stepped forward and said, 'I want to thank Barry, Simon, Jonathan and the boys for a fabulous service and for keeping up. I want to apologise for the damage to the hearse, which I will of course pay for.' This brought a wave of laughter to the proceedings, and I told Paul not to worry. I would not have missed this experience for the world. I had had to learn to blend what the mourners required to cope with their loss, with my own principles and the level of control required.

Every day, my profession brings new situations to learn from. You always have to be ready as the telephone can ring in the middle of the night and change all your best-laid plans. You could find yourself on an oil tanker repatriating seamen after a tragedy, in Cornwall beginning a perfusion for cryonics or, as often happens, just listening to a family who need to open up their grief. Over my working life, I have received the most unusual requests, far beyond what I could ever have imagined.

One distraught man telephoned me after the sad, and premature, death of his daughter with meningitis. I cannot imagine how anyone can cope with such a situation, and this man was looking for any way not to have to let go, especially as another tragedy had left him as both mother and father to her. We talked for hours, shared a drink in his home and looked at every funeral option possible without a definite decision being made. The next day he telephoned to say that he had decided to bury his child in a solid oak coffin with another oak coffin inside, this to be covered with lead and hermetically sealed. This arrangement, called an oak shell and case, has been used for hundreds of years for burials above ground in vaults or in church crypts and is similar to a royal coffin. Albins have always made such coffins, a skill that has never, we are proud to say, been lost even in this age of mass manufacturing.

The burial was to be in a family vault they had just purchased. Modern vaults are quite beautiful, built in the form of a granite mausoleum, each vault containing up to two adults and, in this case, a small child. The father wished to preserve his daughter for all time. Gently embalmed, placed in this coffin with its airtight seal in a dry vault on a fibreglass tray, and then sealed from the air and light, this dear little girl would never change. She would never grow old and would be in her father's mind for ever young.

The day before the funeral, I received a request I had never had before. The father, along with asking for a lock of hair, as many people do, also asked for a DNA sample to be taken. Some time afterwards, I asked him why and he said, 'To this day, Barry, I really don't know. A million thoughts were flashing across my mind; they seem silly now, but I thought, what if I could recreate her, what if she needs it in the future, what if, what if? . . . I just truly wanted to keep so much of her. I didn't want to lose the opportunity; I hope you understand.' When he said this, I knew I had been right not to question his actions at the time as he was trying to deal with his loss by taking such enormous care with his daughter's funeral, paying tribute to her short life. This admirable man has slowly moved on, learning to live alongside his loss and seeing what each new day brings, be it good or bad.

But although I know to expect the unexpected – and learn from it – nothing could have prepared me for a call I received at 10 o'clock one evening. In retrospect, I should not have been so surprised as another funeral director had contacted me the previous day to say he had recommended me: when he had moved a lady from a private address where she had died that morning, her husband had enquired about cryonics but was not sure what exactly he wanted for his wife. As I have had some experience with the technique, my colleague advised him to call me, but even so, I would never have expected what happened next.

I answered the telephone with 'F.A. Albins, Barry speaking; can I help you?' 'No; can you help my wife?', replied a man with a shallow voice. 'She died yesterday,' he explained, 'without letting me know first.' Puzzled, I simply said, 'I'm sorry; where did this happen?'

'At my house, in Clapham.'

'I see. How can I help you?'

'I don't know for sure, but I think I would like to freeze her for ever. Can you do this?'

'Cryonics, yes', I said, 'possibly.'

For about 10 minutes, I explained the procedure of cryonics. When I finished speaking, the man said, 'Yes, maybe. How about freeze-drying?' I had only once heard of freeze-drying – on the television series *LA Law* about five years previously. In the programme, a man had been taken to court because he wanted to freeze-dry his wife and keep her at home. As I did not know how the technique worked or whether or where it could be done, I felt unable to help. The caller then continued, 'Well, how about burning off the skin so I could keep my wife's skeleton at home?' 'No sir. I could not, and would not, be a party to such a procedure. I really can't help you', I responded. 'All right, all right,' he pleaded, 'could you just remove a little skin so

I could cover her favourite Bible and keep it for her grandchildren?' Although I was extremely shocked and disgusted by this suggestion, I kept my cool and simply said no.

By now, I was also rather concerned for the man's health and safety, so I tried to see if he was alone. Moments later, however, he rang off to attend to someone at his front door. Within half an hour, a very kind lady, one of his four daughters, called back to apologise. She explained that the family were not party to any of their father's strange requests and that their mother had, many years before, arranged to donate her body to medical research. This appeared to have angered their father because his wife had, with this request, taken away all his power to choose what type of funeral she should have. This is probably what caused him to consider the most macabre possibilities and might even have pushed him over the edge. 'There but for the grace of God . . .', I thought, but I will never forget his voice as he made his extraordinary requests!

Cases like this show how important it is for people to record their final wishes and leave their estate, however small, properly instructed. One of my hardest, but – I hope – most helpful, responsibilities is that of assisting local families by running a free Will service. Choosing a trustworthy, responsible man or woman to be your executor or executrix is of course one of the most important decisions to be made here. It is often advisable to appoint a solicitor, someone apart from the situation, to administer the Will after death. This may prevent any misunderstanding or bad feeling among the friends and family. The Will must also be witnessed by two independent people. Medical, nursing and hospital staff are always helpful if the person is already in hospital, their act of kindness usually being a great comfort.

The task of preparing the Will itself is not too difficult when all is well. Wills should not be complicated but clear and informative, and local people in good health often enjoy a little light-hearted banter while they are preparing their Will. Some may come back to change it if they fall out with one of the beneficiaries; they then return again to reinstate that person when they have made up. I really enjoy such discussions, so it is neither hard nor laborious to find time to help.

What is really hard though is being involved in writing a Will at what is perhaps the most difficult time of all – shortly before death or at a person's deathbed. But if it is hard for me, how hard is it for the other person, sometimes in pain, always afraid? Even if philosophical, he or she is, whatever their belief, about to embark on an unknown journey. Faith helps, but from the moment we enter this world to the moment we leave it, fear of the unknown is a shadow that never fades. I get a true feeling of contentment from the incredible trust that people place in me. To share someone's most private requests and see clearly the weight being lifted off their shoulders as you help to put their affairs in order is wonderful. It is draining for both of us, and tears are often shed on both sides, but people gather strength from deep inside, a gift we all seem to have when the chips are down.

The courage we find from deep within shows itself in so many different ways, never failing to astound me. I saw this with the case of four children who had been killed in East London. Their short lives had been ended at the hands of their father, who took his own life at the same time. What

10

possessed this man to strap the four children and himself in his silver Nissan car and then set it alight is truly beyond us all. The mother, through her faith and belief in God, showed amazing courage and forgiveness (a better person than me, for sure) as she stood with over 200 mourners at the grave where her four children were laid to rest together, their father placed on his own in a grave alongside.

My whole philosophy as a funeral director is based on trying to be the very best and offer the widest choice of services to all clients and their families. In tragic cases like this, I feel privileged to do even the smallest thing to help. In other instances, the challenge takes a different form. I am often asked about the detail involved in embalming a person who has died; indeed I have always had a great interest in the technique, both in my own professional life and from a historical point of view.

The masters of embalming were of course the Egyptians. The funeral rites experienced by the Egyptians were in truth the centre of all things in those mysterious times, more so than today. The embalmer would have been a well-respected, very rich, popular person, highly in demand. I often wonder whether, like funeral directors today, some were more in demand than others, better at their trade and therefore possessing a popular following. Some of course would have been 'By Royal Appointment' – a frightening experience, with all the responsibility for the departure of a king or queen and the ritual significance of that final journey.

We have to remember that the work of the embalmers of Egyptian times was a labour of love and true belief. The trust in those times in the life of the next world and the importance of the journey across the water to that world, the wealth that was stored for their continuation of life and some of the tombs in which this was stored, along with the mummy itself, were all part of an integral belief that death was only the beginning, a rather different view than the old saying 'You can't take it with you when you go.'

Why, then, was the embalmer so important? After all, if people are going to live on in the next life with the wealth of the current one, why do they need embalming? Embalming today is, I truly believe, as much about protecting the living as preserving the dead, but for the Egyptians it was the opposite. Today we have the three P's – preparation, presentation and preservation – but in ancient Egypt, the sole purpose was the long-term preservation of the body in one whole and complete piece. There was no need to worry about presentation because the body would be wrapped in bandages and sealed in a case. As far as protection was concerned, the Egyptians were undoubtedly aware of the possibility of grave-robbers. After all, it is well documented that tombs were hidden, with concealed entrances and sometimes dummy tombs alongside to protect the true tomb – although they could not have predicted the work of modern archaeologists.

There were different methods of achieving a successful embalming and therefore different standards, linked with costs. Not every mummy embalmed was that of a wealthy person. The afterlife was for all, not just the wealthy, although they would of course rule it. Egyptian embalmers might take many, many months to complete the service they offered. They would have to remove the organs skilfully through the orifices, the organs then being placed in Canopic jars in preservative oil and unrevealed ingredients, concocted by the embalmer, working very closely with the priests. These organs would be replaced or put into the tomb with the mummy so that nothing was lost for the afterlife. The skin would be treated with oils and the body dehydrated. For poorer people, the embalming would have been completed by placing the body in the sun to dry before wrapping it in soaked bandages and burying it. The shell of the body of a wealthy person, now dehydrated, the skin like leather and the organs preserved and hardened, would have been fully and carefully wrapped from tip to toe, each finger and toe swathed individually, to protect the outer shell. The body was then placed into a sarco-phagus, which was sealed. The great and the royal would then have been placed in yet another stone case and sealed with all of their wealth, deep below the earth in rock and Egyptian cement for time immemorial, complete for the journey they believed they would certainly take.

Although I had looked at this process through the history of embalming in my early years of study and travel, I did not get a chance to visit Egypt and the many tombs of the Valley of the Kings until I was 50 years old. It opened a floodgate of thoughts and imaginations, and a better understanding of that history. Most of all, it gave me a greater sense of historical pride in my profession than I had felt before. I could not then have imagined that Albin's Funeral Directors of Bermondsey, in the heart of good old London Town, would be thrown into the world of ancient Egyptian embalming practices and would be forever known as 'Embalmondsey', albeit on the banks of the Thames rather than the Nile. However, having been approached by a respectable gentleman with a request for mummification, I now realise than anything can happen. At an exhibition I once visited in the US, I remember seeing a gold-plated sarcophagus for sale at an unbelievable price. At the time, I truly believed no one would consider this for a modern burial, but after my recent experiences, I am ready to believe that the sarcophagus might find a willing occupant.

The first call came from an old friend of mine, Lee, the excellent superintendent of a local cemetery, whose forward thinking has led him to offer mausoleums and vaults for sale. 'Barry, I know that you are just the man for the job,' he said. 'Thanks, Lee', I replied with some trepidation. He continued, 'I have a client who requires a most unusual service. He sincerely wants you to undertake a mummification, and I have never known you to refuse a genuine client, so what do you think?'

Quite flattered, as Lee knew I would be, I agreed to meet the gentleman the following afternoon. At exactly the appointed hour, the door opened and in leapt Mr Iouannou, with a spring in his step and great expectation in his eyes. 'Mr Barry?', he enquired.

Mr Iouannou, a smiling, modestly dressed man with a Greek accent, seemed kind but excited, extremely nervous but genuine. He was wet and a little cold from his journey across London, but after a cup of tea and a biscuit, he soon warmed up and began to explain. 'Mr Barry, I want to mummify my Mummy. Can this be done?' I told him that I understood exactly what he required, and although I had not undertaken such a case before, I was willing to link some of the past traditions with the science of today and, as he had put it, 'mummify Mum'. In line with my personal philosophy, I wanted to make a complete success of the job and rise to the somewhat unusual occasion.

The lady was in her 80s but looked around 60, with beautiful skin and hair. She must have been a real stunner in her youth. It is all too easy to forget that older people were once young, unmarked by life's journey, and full of hope and expectation. Mark, my young embalmer, and I sat down and planned the work step by step with advice from another five embalmers, in particular Richard Arnold, who helped us to design a concentrated, waterless fluid for the second perfusion after the necessary washout process. After using the concentrated fluid, it was allowed to set at a very low temperature. The Egyptians would have used natron, a naturally occurring compound of sodium carbonate and bicarbonate, to dry the body, with alcohol to kill the bacteria on the skin and then spices, oil resin and asphalt to seal the body. Around the turn of the 20th century, arsenic was the foundation of embalming fluid, but this is no longer used as it proved so deadly to the living handling it.

At this point Mr Iouannou insisted on viewing his mother in private to say goodbye in his own way. She looked very peaceful as we laid her on a bed in a chapel to follow her faith in the Greek Orthodox style. As Mr Iouannou and his mother both had a deep faith in the Greek Orthodox Church, he was delighted with this. It was clear that his mother was his whole life, and her loss was devastating. His wanting to preserve her in such a fashion, although rarely practised and viewed as strange today, was an attempt, I believe, to preserve for ever her existence in this world. Maybe at the back of his mind also lay the early Christian idea that to enter heaven, the body would have to be whole and not cremated. Indeed it was not, I believe, until the 1950s that the Pope gave permission for Catholics to be cremated, and even today many Catholics still prefer burial.

After viewing his mother, Mr Iouannou requested some photos to keep as a record: 'Thank you, Mr Barry,' he cried, 'these are very important to me. You see, Mummy will be beautiful forever. God bless you and your people for that.' Moments like that, when you know your vocation is clear and correct, never leave you.

Over the next few days, we completed the preparation and were now ready to seal the skin with a special ointment and wrap the body in the first layer of bandages, also photographing this stage. When the body had set hard, it was placed in a vacuum bag and the air was removed. The bag was then put into a pouch and sealed with hot glue, airtight and ready for sealing in the two coffins, or sarcophagi, whichever term you prefer. The outer coffin was special solid, seasoned two-inch oak, dovetailed and dowelled, into which was placed a solid metal inner coffin that was then hermetically sealed. The outer lid of the wooden coffin was hot-fastened with sealer, wood dowels and top screws.

Perhaps the nicest thing for me was the Greek Orthodox Church service and the blessing of the vault at the cemetery, both moving and sincere. Will someone in a thousand years' time open the coffin, sitting on its fibreglass tray in perfect condition in a sealed vault and wonder what story lies behind it?

The whole experience was quite strange, and my mind wandered a lot during the work. Looking at the mummy wrapped in its first layer of soaked bandages, I found myself back in the 1960s watching the television show *The Invisible Man*. In it, an experiment by scientist Peter Brady went horribly wrong, and he became permanently invisible. At the time, we thought this was great: if he smoked, all you would see was a cigar and some smoke rings; if there was no one in the seat next to us at school, we would say Peter Brady was sitting there. The real resemblance though came from the bandages he wrapped around his head, looking just like a mummy, but then he would spoil it by putting a hat and sunglasses on. It would often lead to us joking at school when there was a knock at the door, shouting, 'If that's the invisible man, tell him I can't see him'. Memories of my school days passed in a moment, bringing me quickly back to the reality of Mr Iouannou's mother and the required dignity of her procedure.

Mr Iouannou kept a little of his mum's hair and those precious photographs. He and I know that there are no guarantees for the work, and neither of us will be around to stand over them, but we shared the same enthusiasm to be successful in this venture, and that, and his trust in our ability, is what really counts. Mr Iouannou confided in me that he may one day take his mother back to Greece and place her in her family tomb, hoping to be with her himself at a later point. So just as a little of the Egyptian way of final departures has visited Bermondsey, so too may a little of Bermondsey rest in the East and complete the circle.

2
The best possible taste?

A trip back in time to ancient Egypt was not something I had expected to encounter in my work, but as a funeral director you never know who or what will greet you when the phone rings. Some of the situations I have encountered have been extraordinary, some bizarre, some, to me, just tasteless. We all have limits to what we will find acceptable, and maybe a look at some of the more unusual or despicable incidents surrounding death will give us an idea of where we stand.

I know the power of love is great and that we need to keep those we love close to us, but a lady in Australia went a step further when her husband, a 50-year-old businessman, died suddenly in a tragic car accident. A colleague of mine was asked to undertake the cremation, after which he received an unusual request from the widow that the ashes should be ground as small as possible and forwarded to a breast enhancement clinic in Sydney. It seems that the widow had arranged for the ashes of her beloved husband to be stitched into her breast implants so that, in her own words, he could be close to her heart. To me, this certainly seems a little extreme!

It is not only the families of those who have died who have unusual ways of doing things. One funeral director in Missouri, US, for example, had a very strange way of collecting a bad debt. After he had removed the deceased from the hospital, as instructed by the family in preparation for the burial, there was, it seems, a change of heart, and the family said that they would not pay for this. In anger, the undertaker decided to return the deceased – simply enclosed in a see-through, blue plastic bag. But he did not leave it at the hospital or even the public mortuary; instead, he deposited it on the doorstep of the family home for all to see. However much the family should have kept to their side of the contract, such behaviour is not acceptable; it is cruel and of course unprofessional. Needless to say, the undertaker had his licence suspended.

A number of corpses in Ohio had their final departure interrupted by an unscrupulous deputy coroner and his assistant as they allowed their enthusiasm for photography to get the better of them. They were found guilty in a court of law of unzipping body bags and then, to the disgust of the rest of society, putting the bodies in so-called artistic positions with apples, keys and other inappropriate objects, in order to obtain private photographs of the dead. These photographs became their final undoing, and the deceased people unwillingly involved went respectfully to their ends, albeit with less dignity as a result of this despicable behaviour.

This is not the only time that art has been used as an excuse for unseemly behaviour. Whitechapel in London, the past scene of many murders by Jack the Ripper, was home to an exhibition of body parts, called Bodyworlds. This housed exactly what the name suggests – real body parts – from foetal remains to fully exposed male and female bodies. It is truly remarkable that anyone could conceive such a project, let alone produce it. One can only assume that, unlike the unwilling participants in Ohio, the subjects of this exhibition gave their consent. Although I would be the first to agree that people have the right to choose to pledge their bodies for the future, I am not sure that a public exhibition of the dead is a suitable forum. Although I can admire the incredible work of preservation that has been undertaken, and feel that this is artistically quite brilliant in its concept, it seems an unnecessary and undignified way to treat people. It makes me wonder whether the incredible body parts I have seen in medical museums, probably donated for medical research, are not there just out of morbid curiosity. There seems to be a thin line here between education and ghoulishness.

Another act of extraordinary preservation was undertaken by Robert Leniewicz 1941–2002 (aged 60); painter, draughtsman, artist; very clever fellow; an incredible man who lived a strange and varied life and could turn his hand to almost anything. He once housed 700 tramps in nine warehouses, and when he died, the embalmed remains of a down and out named Edwin McKenzie were found in one of his drawers. It seems that McKenzie signed a contract with Leniewicz in 1978 so that, when McKenzie died in November 1984, Leniewicz had him fully embalmed and then hid him in the drawer. The public health authority tried to claim the body, but Leniewicz would not disclose its current whereabouts; in fact, he had not broken any law by what he did. And what next - will the administrator of Leniewicz's belongings claim the body to be a piece of art and thus of value to the estate? At the moment, the Plymouth coroner is the keeper of McKenzie's body until the High Court decides what to do with it. Poor Edwin McKenzie was as unlucky in death as he had been in life.

Macabre happenings are of course not limited to the UK. One of the most morbid scenes I have ever witnessed is at the Capuchin Church in Rome. The order of monks there has converted the old bonery into what was to me a chamber of horrors - a freak show. They had made patterns from all types of bone and, if my memory serves me well, hung skeletons on the walls and ceiling, and stacked them in some kind of designer show. Some were even varnished. The old monk in charge of the Church insisted on a financial contribution from all who entered and handed out booklets asking for a further payment. These bones had once all been human beings whose life had meaning; in death, they would have been honoured as Christians honour their dead, but now they had become merely ornaments.

Another place where the dead are disconcertingly on view is a tunnel in Mexico, built directly through a chamber of catacombs. Here none of the bodies that were in the way of the digging were moved - they were simply placed on the tunnel wall. As you drive through, the bones and parts of bodies embalmed like leather are all around, both a memory of the past and a reminder of everyone's certain future. I can only hope that this bizarre display will be a stunning reminder to people to drive safely and not a distraction.

All these unusual experiences raise for me so many questions of right and wrong, acceptable and unacceptable. If these instances are wrong, do we need to look at others in the same way? What about the catacombs in Rome or Sardinia, the museums housing bodies from the Ice Age, mummies from ancient Egypt and relics of early man? The dead as they lie in Pompeii still preserved by the volcanic lava, and the bodies of saints and famous people – such as Lenin – are all viewed daily by tourists, believers, worshippers, scientists and even our children in the name of education. These things are available to us because we request to see them, so maybe it is society that is truly bizarre rather than the people who display these artefacts. As we open our minds up, where does the difference between modern displays and past history lie? Will, for instance, Bodyworlds become part of our descendants' history lessons? The only certainty seems to be a universal inner curiosity about death.

Not all displays of death are, however, quite so despicable. Again in Mexico, as well as in some other countries around the globe, they hold a wonderful Day of the Dead. People hold this day in huge regard and accept it as a festival of thanksgiving for their ancestors. It is based on the Catholic belief in the life ever after. Thousands of Masses for the dead are celebrated, with a little pagan tradition, as in most old rituals. Members of each family carry a small skeleton, usually in a case and often clothed, which brings good luck. On this special day, families join together from all over Mexico, bringing food, candles and music for a vast, 24-hour celebration and vigil for the dead. Although this may seem bizarre, it is really a caring and healthy way to deal with death.

You might be happy to celebrate in a Mexican street carrying a model of a skeleton, but would you buy the house of your dreams if it came with an urn containing the ashes of the last owner, displayed in a prominent position on the mantelpiece for all to see? The dear old man in question loved his house in Pimlico in London so much that he could not allow even death to part him from it. Written into his Will was the statement that he must remain on the mantelpiece as long as the house remained standing and that any future sale – of a very desirable Georgian terraced property near Victoria station – was to include the urn and ashes displayed in a prominent position as a fixture and fitting. How content he must have been in his 70 years on this earth to want to remain in his everyday surroundings.

This reminds me of the film *Meet the Parents*, in which Robert De Niro plays a retired CIA agent who is very possessive of his daughter and wary of any boyfriend she brings home. On the mantelpiece, he keeps an urn of his mother's ashes, his pride and joy and loving keepsake – until his daughter's fiancé visits for the first time. After De Niro has recited a poem to his late mother, the terrified fiancé opens a bottle of champagne in her honour, popping the cork with incredible speed and cracking the urn. The ashes fall to the ground, only to be treated like cat litter by the beloved household pet!

As you will see throughout this book, I am a great one for old films and television shows. For me, *I Love Lucy* was a comedy classic from the 1950s and 60s, but for the husband of a recently departed Lucy the phrase meant so much more. Jeff, Lucy's husband, was a 32-year-old American living in Arizona, who, because of the grief he suffered at her death, acted totally out of character and not in a way we would expect of any 'sane' person. But, as I said at the beginning of the chapter, we must always remember that grief arising from bereavement is a powerful adversary and can cause all sorts of extraordinary behaviour.

Lucy had been born with a heart condition that cut her life short at the tender age of just 29 years. Deeply in love, Lucy's last words were, 'We will meet again in heaven', but those words were no consolation to Jeff, who could feel only total despair. At the funeral, he made a final decision that he could not let Lucy leave him so instead of accepting closure (an American term for the end of the grieving experience) and a final interment for Lucy, he brought her home and began to make extraordinary arrangements. First, Jeff contacted the cemetery superintendent, then the funeral director, and then the relevant authorities. Finally, having had a premier embalming of Lucy (an intensive, long, preservative procedure of embalming), he ordered a special hermetically sealed glass case that helps to eliminate decomposition of the dead body. If the case is correctly vacuum sealed, no air will enter it.

Jeff's proposal was, 'Lucy had a great sense of humour, and I'm sure she would appreciate being my coffee table in the lounge', surely a completely macabre idea. All this cost Jeff around $6000, providing him with not just Lucy's new resting place, but also, to him, a fine piece of furniture. 'People thought it very strange, but the authorities could find no real reason to refuse: sealed in that case and embalmed, there would be no health risk,' said Jeff. 'Some relatives and friends, filled with trepidation, stopped visiting us,' (note here his use of the word 'us', seeming to deny that the real Lucy is no longer with him) 'but my true friends just respected my decision and continued to visit us both; some even comment how great it looks.' You can judge for yourself in the photograph that my American colleague Carole has sent me. But is this so very different from the ashes on the mantelpiece in Pimlico? Or from Lenin on show to the whole world, as I describe in the next chapter? Again, this provides food for thought in setting the boundaries of how we treat those who have died. It also reminds us true love means letting go, as I'm sure Jeff would once have known too.

Although embalming has been around since time immemorial, I often think it strange that it took a civil war to create the opportunity for modern embalming to develop. Thomas Holmes, considered by Americans to be the father of scientific arterial embalming, learnt his craft and was able to exercise his skill and develop his fluids throughout the American Civil War of 1861–65. He was a good and thoughtful man who devoted endless hours to embalming the young soldiers who lost their lives in battle – he knew the importance of returning these soldiers to their homes and families. It was reported that he embalmed many hundreds of soldiers and placed them in graves or tunnels underneath a river, where they remained in an excellent condition throughout the course of the war, before going home to be seen by their loved ones. This is a true and touching story; as far as I am concerned, the only bizarre happening here is the Civil War itself.

An equally interesting instance of mass embalming can also be found in the tiny Egyptian village of Ain Labakha, west of the River Nile. Here, among the wealthy corpses of the Pharaohs and other dignitaries, lie the Tombs of the

Poor, dating back over 2000 years. All those buried here had a hard life and died young from harsh conditions, malnutrition and the effects of hard physical labour. The 60 mummies, lying side by side, were embalmed by dehydration and the simple, old techniques I described in Chapter 1: no matter how poor a person was, it was equally important to maintain the body in one piece so that it could be reunited with the soul in the next world.

With no riches to steal, this amazing find had been left undisturbed until recently. But we are the most enquiring civilisation of all time, so the bodies – still with clear features and their hair intact – were X-rayed and logged before being kindly returned to their grave just as they were found. Lying far from the tourist trail, they will hopefully be able to rest together for ever now that they have given up so many of their secrets.

But as well as being inquisitive, people are great inventors, so here's a new way to go – freeze-drying. It seems that this could soon be a reality in Sweden. It is reported to be a very 'green' solution to disposing of the dead as the corpse is turned into fertiliser after being freeze-dried and shattered: 'From earth we came, to the earth we will return', as it is written. Invented by the Swedish ecologist Susanne Wiigh-Masak, this technique has so far been tested only on dead pigs and cows, but it is hoped that it will soon be applied to human remains. Wiigh-Masak believes the cost will be comparable to that of cremation. As I am not a fan of cremation, I doubt I would like freeze-drying any better but, if it were done with dignity, care and a funeral so that everyone could say goodbye, I could see it as being acceptable.

In the same way that we have a right to choose freeze-drying if we want, surely we also have a right to choose burial or cremation? Not necessarily, it seems. A woman weighing 22 stone was recently refused cremation in Scotland. It seems that her coffin was about two inches larger than the average crematorium oven (which is some 30 or 31 inches wide), so cremation is apparently not possible for such large people. How bizarre that 'sizeism' is a notable prejudice in life – we make large clothes, large shoes, large seats – yet we do not expect larger people to die and require cremation.

And what about transport to our final resting place? Do you like motorcycles? Could you visualise your final departure in a side-car? Well, it now seems that that *is* possible. Reverend Paul Sinclair has become the ultimate 'final dispatcher' on his remarkably designed but fully enclosed motorcycle side-car hearse. Paul loves motorcycles and wanted sincerely to provide this option for all those who shared his passion. He has thought of everything in his excellent design – a place for flowers, a roof rack, trestles for the coffin to stand on, space for cleaning materials, a full interior bier and stops for the coffin. What an inventive and unusual kick start to the next world! Two other enthusiasts, Bill Tanner and Tony Crathern, have designed and built a trailer hearse with bier and roof rack for flowers, which is towed behind a beautiful three-wheeled, two-seater Harley Davidson motorbike. They advertise this for hire as 'The Final Ride'.

A funeral director in West London for me holds the record for the most amusing motor hearse of all time. He has converted a Robin Reliant three-wheeler, just like the one Del Boy drives in the television series *Only Fools and Horses*, which he says he uses for mortuary collections and local funerals – as long as the deceased is not too tall or too heavy. It reminds me of that old song I used to hear at Millwall Football Club when I was a kid: 'three wheels on my wagon, and I'm still rolling along'!

Although we rely on a range of technology to help in dealing with the departed, it is often not all quite as useful as the motor vehicle. Pacemakers, for example, are a godsend to the living but a nightmare for the funeral director and a direct danger to the cremation operator. The funeral industry is of course fully aware of the problem and takes all precautions to avoid untoward happenings, but even many doctors I have met have not known that a pacemaker can cause an explosion, endangering staff and damaging ovens. This occurs when the pacemaker is subjected to immediate and intense heat, causing a reaction between the chemicals it contains or leading to a release of stored energy. (I should stress here that pacemakers are of no danger whatsoever to people who have them fitted successfully during their lifetime, whatever the daily temperature.)

Since 1976, when the first explosion occurred at a crematorium, the medical powers that be changed the cremation forms to add a question on the removal of pacemakers and thus ensure safety for all concerned. The pacemaker can itself be easily removed by the doctor, a trained nurse or an embalmer. It is interesting to note at this point that, in accordance with the original Cremation Act of 1902, making a false entry on the required documentation leads to a penalty of imprisonment. Fortunately, explosions now rarely occur, thanks to vigilance, professionalism and the correct controls.

I have tried to describe all these interesting, unusual, bizarre and despicable happenings with sensitivity and a little light-heartedness, hoping that they will open all our minds to the many issues involved in remembering that people have a right to choose their method of final departure without being the victims of too much judgement. But some situations are so horrifying that they can never be acceptable, as we will see now in my last story.

In the US, funeral directors are tested for a licence by state law in a vigorous examination of their knowledge, respectability and professionalism that is second to none. They require excellent premises and have to abide by very strict rules and guidelines, otherwise they will be in danger of losing their licence and therefore their business. The same rules apply to embalmers (known as juicers) and reconstruction artists (some of whom are also embalmers) so you would think that the industry is well governed. This is not, however, true in the case of cremation: at least 10 states have no laws at all, and most of the states that do have laws do not enforce them adequately. It seems that cremation is seriously under-regulated at every level.

In the UK, funerals are arranged similarly whether they are burials or cremations – the same process of a church or chapel, a service, cars and flowers, albeit with a different end. In the US, though, it is very different. Anyone seems to be able to open what they call a 'crematory', these being very different from the crematoriums of the UK or Europe. In the UK, crematoriums are mostly owned by the local authorities or private companies; either way, they abide by very strict rules and are carefully monitored. The crematorium receives a deceased person, always safely in a fastened coffin with the correct paperwork, which has been double-checked by an independent medical referee 48 hours before. The crematorium then undertakes to complete the cremation on the same day, this being a rule and requirement, however late in the day it might be. On completion of the cremation, the bones are removed and ground to ash, placed in a new urn and registered for scattering, burial, removal by the family or whatever is the final requirement.

But in the US, the crematory is usually a small facility that is privately run, sometimes by a funeral director, although many are run by unregulated operators and are small, out-of-the-way and rarely checked facilities. Cremation, which about 25 per cent of Americans choose, compared with 71 per cent of the UK population, is very poorly viewed by American funeral directors as there is little for them to do and the income from cremation is very small. Their only task is to remove the deceased, with the death certificate, in a cardboard box to one of these facilities. The family may then have a memorial service with or without the ashes, but the funeral director does not really represent the funeral in the same way. A crematory family facility may serve many funeral homes in the area. The funeral director will drop off the deceased and a few days later collect the ashes to return them to the family or wherever is required.

In the hamlet of Noble, Georgia, US, however, this was far from what happened. In February 2002, the Tri-State Crematory, a company offering a cremation service to the funeral directors in the local vicinity as a subcontractor, was investigated by the Environment Protection Agency after an anonymous telephone call. It was their second visit after a tip-off over a period of three months. This time, as well as just talking to the owner, they searched the area. What they found was to shock and disgust the world. The first horrific find was a human skull, further investigation unearthing piles of human remains stacked one on top of the other. Some were in a creek, others in a shed or under leaves; even the wells had to be tested for contamination. Approximately 300 bodies were spread around the area; as the bodies were being collected and identified, all that could be seen from an aeroplane flying overhead were rows and rows of white body bags, all full. There were even full, rusty coffins that must have been used for cremation a long time previously and had just been left to rot above ground. The only explanation offered by the operator, Ray Brent Marsh, was that the incinerator was broken.

Despite a lifetime in the funeral business, I have never experienced or heard of such a sickening and unbelievable practice. How could this happen? To this man, the body certainly was not sacred. He could not have cared less what happened. Families who had thought they had said goodbye to their loved one, and accepted closure, a long time ago now had to face the terrifying reality that the cremation had never been completed and that the ashes they had received were just woodchip and dust, their loved ones simply being stacked in a pile with other remains. The children in one family could not understand how Nanny could be in two places at once: in the urn they had and in the woods. Their mother's answer was simple: 'Somebody has lied to us.' Relatives sent urns full of ashes back for testing in order to set their minds at rest.

With great justification, hundreds of angry people packed the crematory wanting to know whether their loved one was one of those left so cruelly to rot. I have heard so many sad stories from the US concerning families facing up to the true horror of this situation and trying just to find their loved ones. The Red Cross, dentists, pathologists, the state police, funeral directors and volunteers took part in the clean-up and identification of the bodies, with counsellors and church ministers on hand to help.

I am amazed that of the 30 or so funeral homes that used the crematory when they delivered the deceased and, a few days later, collected the ashes in a plastic urn, none ever seemed to have checked the ashes or smelt the decay in the area. Or was it a funeral director who informed the authorities? Whatever the truth, I cannot understand how this carried on over such a long period.

The operator has, of course, been arrested, but final charges have still to be made and lawsuits will undoubtedly ensue. I just hope that whatever sentence he may face, living with himself will be one equal to what he has imposed on those poor families, whose damage can never be repaired. For those who have died, I pray that their final departure will be completed with some deserved dignity. Thank God that such despicable happenings are so rare.

3
Departures of the famous

All that is
is forever:
only the shell
fades away

I have always had a particular interest in the funerals of the famous, past and present, and take every opportunity to research the details or even to visit the actual places where some amazing final departures have taken place. Having conducted my fair share of high-profile funerals, such as those of the actor Donald Pleasance and the murdered Peckham schoolboy Damilola Taylor, I am fascinated to learn how my colleagues from around the world have coped with some of the biggest funerals of all time and the added pressure of being in the spotlight themselves.

In the late 1980s, I attended the American Convention of Funeral Directors in New Orleans. For me it was a great adventure. I had just been appointed as European Agent

35

for Airline Mortuary Services (AMS), the world-famous repatriation service and part of Continental and Eastern Airlines. This was a real coup for me and very exciting. I went first to the head office of AMS in Houston, Texas, to join my friend John Baumber, the general manager of AMS. It was there that I was to meet Carole Bearden, an AMS manager who would later become a soulmate, one of those rare people you realise will always be a special friend. Carole had been appointed to look after me throughout my visit. On the way to stay at her family home, we stopped to watch her son Kenny playing in a little league baseball game. How fascinating to see American culture, with all its passion, at such close range. The next evening, however, I realised what a dangerous place it really could be when Carole insisted I lock my car door while we were driving through the centre of New Orleans. But I was treated to breakfast at Flanagan's and an evening of amaretto sours in the French Quarter, which was quite an experience.

At the convention, too, I was to meet some amazing people: casket manufacturers, navy, army and airforce personnel, mortuary service operators, organ manufacturers, vehicle-makers – you name them, I met them. All totally focused on looking after people's final journeys. To these people, there was no such thing as 'Mind your own business' as everybody and anybody was their business – dead or alive!

Being in New Orleans, I had expected to meet some French funeral directors, and I was not disappointed. I bumped into some old friends, Patrick and Pierre, from my many dealings with the Parisian funeral industry, and they introduced me to one of the retired directors of their firm: 'An interesting but strange man', they giggled. This man stood about six feet tall with round shoulders, grey hair, glasses and a strange American accent with French under-tones. He was smoking a small cigar and wore a badly pressed suit. He paid little attention to me – a non-French speaking, young would-be world funeral director – and seemed to be in a hurry to leave. As my curiosity was aroused, I asked my friends what position this man had held in his day. 'We will let you into a little secret', they said. 'This man bought the first funeral home for the company outside France.' How strange, I thought, to buy one funeral home so far away: it is probably not cost-effective, and you have no knowledge of the local customs and little control over the operation of the business. Trusting people in such a situation could prove very difficult. But Patrick and Pierre went on to explain. 'The funeral home he purchased was in Memphis, Tennessee, we only owned it for a while, and it was a disaster.' 'Why?', I asked. 'Well,' they replied, 'they took our money and then took advantage of our lack of local knowledge. In simple terms, no one gave a damn. There is a tale that when Elvis Presley died, the funeral home declined the funeral because they were busy!' Needless to say, they no longer own the funeral home. Fancy turning down the funeral of one of the most famous entertainers of all time, if this is what actually happened. But this set me off thinking about Elvis Presley's funeral and who had actually conducted it.

The King: Elvis Aaron Presley (1935–1977)

'I won't' were the last words that Elvis was to murmur on the 16th August 1977. Elvis died sitting on a black leather chair in his bathroom, reading a book about the Turin Shroud, the possible burial gown of Christ. Elvis was 42 years of age and a legend; his funeral was to be one that Memphis, indeed the world, would never forget. Graceland, Elvis' home at 3764 Elvis Presley Boulevard, has now become a shrine for all time.

At the time of Elvis' death, there was pandemonium, over 3000 people gathering at Graceland in great confusion. We do not really know what happened about the French funeral directors, but I suspect that the funeral was really always going to be conducted by the Memphis Funeral Home, one of the largest and most respected funeral homes in Tennessee and owned by the company, Service Corporation International (SCI): Randal M. Max Snow, vice president and general manager of the home, had previously arranged the funeral of Elvis' mother in August 1958. Within hours of Elvis' death, there were security guards posted at the gate of the funeral home. With the gates now locked, the 45 employees prepared to undertake probably their biggest challenge yet. The switchboard was alight with calls. Most were enquiries, but some were messages to be passed on to Elvis from his fans, such was this man's popularity.

Elvis was to be buried in the same design of casket that he had previously chosen for his mother, a silver-plated, national seamless copper casket. This large casket had to be flown in on a private jet from the Halin-Cook Funeral Home in Oklahoma City, another branch of the SCI group. Elvis was embalmed and dressed in a white suit, a light blue silk shirt and a matching white cashmere tie. His personal hairdresser, Larry Geller, styled his hair and coloured some grey areas jet black. Elvis was now ready to be laid in state at Graceland. So many flowers were sent there that florists had to be drafted in to help the local outlets, the flower markets were sold out and blooms had to be brought in from other areas of the US. Had the funeral been in Bermondsey, I'm sure it would have closed everything for a week – definitely 'all shook up'.

After a private family viewing, the casket was covered with some 500 roses, and a queue a mile long was slowly allowed to view the body. On 18th August, the Governor of Mississippi ordered a state day of mourning, and all flags were ordered to fly half-mast for the funeral. Early on the morning of the service, which was held at Graceland, a fleet of vans transferred the flowers to the cemetery where Elvis' mother had been laid to rest in the family mausoleum. The service resounded with stirring gospel music and wonderful eulogies to Elvis' memory. After the final family viewing, Elvis' famous large gold ring, with its black onyx face and small cluster of diamonds, was finally removed.

Elvis loved cars, especially Cadillacs, and would have loved the funeral cortège – 16 white Cadillacs, white being 'his' colour at that time. At the end of Elvis Presley Boulevard, another 50 cars carrying other guests followed the cortège, led by three police motorcycle outriders, for the slow journey to the cemetery. The roads were lined with tearful fans and press and television crews from around the world. There were flowers in the shape of a crown, guitars, teddy bears, a broken heart and blue suede shoes, all depicting the great man and his music.

The final committal took place at the ornate family mausoleum and lasted for only 10 minutes. A friend of mine, a funeral director who was privileged to be an eye witness to the events, said that the family and friends left the grave, leaving Elvis' father Vernon behind. Vernon knew what was to follow: for Elvis, this was not his final departure as there was to be a loving but very low-profile return departure to Graceland. Under cover of darkness at 7 p.m. on 25th September, the bodies of Elvis and his mother were removed, with only Vernon and the funeral directors (all 14 of them) in attendance, to two beautiful vaults in the Garden of Meditation at Graceland. Elvis had such a powerful aura that there are people who still believe he is alive, or has been abducted by aliens, but for me Elvis has definitely 'left the building'.

Elvis, like so many people who have the ability to change the world, died well before his time. Maybe their energy extinguishes life's flame when it burns so brightly, or maybe they have just given all they can in this life and are truly ready to move on. But such individuals always live on in what they have left behind. My son, who was not even born when Elvis died, loves his music. Even the local Chinese restaurant in New Cross, London, is called Graceland, the owner performing nightly as a Chinese Elvis impersonator. Surely that is proof enough of the man's power?

That'll Be the Day that I Die: Buddy Holly (1936–1959)

The same could be said of the legendary rock 'n' roller Buddy Holly. Born Charles Holly, his short life was already over by the time I was 8 years old, but such was the magic of his music that my whole generation was motivated by the songs he left with us forever.

On 2nd February 1959 (coincidentally my birthday),

Buddy boarded a light aircraft with two other amazing musicians, J.P. Richardson (the Big Bopper) and Richard Valenzuela (better known as Ritchie Valence), as well as the pilot, Roger Peterson. But they were never to step off the plane. Don McLean commemorated 'the day the music died' in his famous song *American Pie*.

Buddy was the first person I remember being repatriated for his funeral. Employees from the Wilcox and Ward Van Slyke funeral homes were first summoned to remove the bodies, Buddy being taken to the Van Slyke home to be embalmed by Mr Van Slyke in preparation for his return to Lubbock, Texas. On 4th February, a specially chartered plane arrived to collect Buddy. His brother and his brother-in-law, J.E. Weir, travelled to accompany him on his return (escorting the deceased being common practice in the US). A bad storm had caused Buddy's plane to crash in the first place, and, ironically, it was a bad storm that delayed his return to Lubbock for 24 hours.

Buddy eventually returned to the Saunders Funeral Home in Lubbock in preparation for his funeral service on 7th February. Saunders Funeral Home was, and still is, a well-run home with strong family connections and a very friendly professional touch. In Buddy's time, it was furnished in traditional 1950s style and very homely. The service itself took place at 2 p.m. at the Tabernacle Baptist Church in Lubbock, with 1500 mourners to say goodbye. These were led by Buddy's wife, Maria Elena, the service being conducted by the Reverend Ben D. Johnson, who had married the couple only five months before. Some of Buddy's favourite gospel songs – *Beyond the Sunset* and *I'll Be Alright* – were played but, strangely, none of Buddy's own material. On a day that it really was 'raining in everybody's heart', hearing those words from Buddy would have been perfect.

After the service, the 18-gauge steel casket was taken to the Lubbock City Cemetery for burial. Buddy's headstone is a simple flat marker inscribed with the words 'In Loving Memory of our own Buddy Holly September 7 1936 – February 3 1959' and a raised carving of Buddy's electric guitar. In Clear Lake, the site of the crash, is a small marker, and every year on 3rd February, fans from all over the world come to the Surf Ballroom for a concert to remember the three singers. The great Sir Paul McCartney paid the highest tribute of all when he purchased the rights to Buddy's music.

John Winston Lennon
(later John Winston Ono Lennon; 1940–1980)

From one great Beatle to another. It is said that everyone can remember where they were when John F. Kennedy was shot, and the same can be said of John Lennon, such was the fame of this great musician.

John was shot dead on 8th December 1980 as he and his wife Yoko were arriving at their New York apartment. They had earlier in the day been stopped by the man we now know as Mark Chapman, who had asked for an autograph when they were leaving to put the finishing touches to one of Yoko's records. Later, as the couple got out of their limousine and walked to their apartment, Mark Chapman pulled out a gun and fired five shots into John's back and shoulder; he then dropped the empty gun to the floor, pulled out a copy of the American cult book *Catcher in the Rye* (which I worked through at school and never understood) and began to read it. The police arrested Mark Chapman, placed John in the back of the patrol car and asked him, 'Do you know who you are?' He moaned, nodded his head and said no more. John Winston Ono Lennon died hours later in the emergency room of the Roosevelt Hospital after a massive loss of blood.

Unlike Elvis, John was to be cremated without fuss or delay. But no one could have expected so many people to crowd the streets around the funeral home for this simple service of cremation, and no one could have predicted the next amazing happenings. Fans came from everywhere to place flowers and lighted candles at the spot where he had died. His music was played continuously on the radio and wherever people gathered, all over the world. They had to block 72nd Street as the fans would not go home, instead singing and chanting two of John's last songs, *Give Peace a Chance* and *Imagine*. John's departure was really made final only after Yoko asked for a silent vigil, impeccably respected, to be held on 14th December at 2 p.m. The world had been robbed of John's greatness. We all have to face death, we all have our time, but for so many, this should not have been John's. As for Mark Chapman, he said that 'only by killing the "bad" [external] John could he get on with his own life as the "good" [internal] John.' But John himself, like Elvis, still lives on in the hearts of others, songs like *Imagine* being regularly played at many other funerals.

I visited the place where John was shot, as well as the famous Frank E. Campbell Funeral Home in New York, and have spoken to the funeral directors who cared for him. Ironically, Eugene Schultz, the vice president and later president of the funeral home, was just around the corner at the time of John's shooting, having been specially requested to remove a deceased person from another building. He remembered hearing all the sirens and the commotion but did not know what had happened until the next morning. As Campbell's are *the* funeral home in New York City, they can truly expect to be called for 90 per cent of funerals of the famous, so the press had already made camp at the home's entrance. As they had expected, Yoko arrived, on 10th December at 11 a.m., to plan John's cremation, a private service whose plans were not to be disclosed.

Campbell's picked up John's body on a covered, one-man stretcher and removed it to the funeral home, along with all the necessary documents for cremation. Needless to say, word got out that John's body was at Campbell's, and the surrounding streets became crowded with photographers, reporters, fans and people who just simply wanted to be at this historical occasion. By now, the body had been made ready and put in a simple casket, which was placed on a hearse at the rear of the building with only the driver in attendance. The hearse left, followed by a crowd of press and other vehicles. But what no one knew was that the hearse was a decoy and the casket an empty case. About 20 minutes later, the real hearse and escort left with John quietly for a private cremation at Ferncliff Crematorium and Cemetery in Westchester County, New York. The decoy hearse returned, press in tow, about 30 minutes later – a job well done! Standing in the large reception of the Campbell Funeral Home, I could sense the company's importance and fully understand why people turn to them for the final departures of the New York famous.

A number of years previously, my family and I had visited

the land of the Beatles; well, we all loved their music so much. We were taken round to see the site of The Cavern Club, Strawberry Fields, Penny Lane and where John lived with his Aunt Mimi. Being a Liverpool Football Club supporter, this was doubly special. When I later stood on the spot where John Lennon died, my mind flew from scene to scene, as in a play, my imagination protecting me from the reality of what had actually happened. But, as with any death, the truth eventually hit me right in the face – that John Lennon had gone. He will of course continue to reach out to future generations as he has done to those past and present. In the words of the also-immortal William Shakespeare:

> We are such stuff as dreams are made on
> and our little life is rounded with a sleep.

Peter Alexeevich, Czar of All Russia (1672–1725)

It is not just the rich and famous of our own times who leave a mark on us by their passing. All I had ever known about Peter Alexeevich, or Peter the Great, was that he was Russian, but all that changed when a friend of mine, a minister, became deeply involved in the history of Czar Peter, his passion rubbing off on everyone around him.

Peter, a huge, fit, young man who stood over 6 feet 8 inches in height, but with a very small head, originally came to Deptford in South London to learn about ship-building so that he could return to Russia and build a navy. He was a far-sighted man with many skills – diplomacy, science, carpentry – but most of all he was a great leader and not afraid of hard work.

Where does an undertaker in Bermondsey come into this, you may ask. Well, it seems that while learning to build ships, Peter learned a new skill, coffin-building. In Russia, the approach was to cut down a whole tree and scrape out the centre to create a coffin, a terrible waste, but Peter learned, from local Deptford coffin-makers and carpenters, how to make many coffins from just one tree by joining and sealing. When made, the coffin would be covered in a woollen material and decorated with metal pins and studs, as was the tradition at that time. Many of the coffins were then lined with a second coffin covered in lead and sealed so that they protected the body for crypt burials. Peter took this skill back to Russia and changed the whole concept of wood use and coffin-making.

Perhaps even more important for Peter was his meeting with the Petts family (as in Petts Wood in South London). The Petts family were great tree-planters, cultivators and land-owners in the South London and Kent borders, and held the contract to supply the wood that built the British Navy. As Peter's original plan was of course to build up a Russian navy, he took their knowledge back with him and began to plant, correctly, many forests to produce the timber that would be needed.

When this remarkable man died on 28th January 1725, he was mourned by all Russia. He was, after all, probably their greatest son, their Emperor and Czar. He never nominated an heir, as was tradition: he had in fact executed the eldest of his 11 children, Czarevich Alexei, for treason. Peter was obviously not a man to be messed with in life – or in death. His final departure in St Petersburg would have been a splendid affair of state. The nation mourned Peter like no previous leader before him. Despite Peter's ruthless, cold nature, the nation saw only the good, and loved Peter, so public grief was sincere. State funerals are of course not just a show of grief, but also a show of strength, representation from the armed forces in procession depicting a nation in mourning and a warning to the outside world. Peter's funeral would have also been an affair of the people, the streets lined many-deep. Foreign royal families and dignitaries would have been present too. Closing our eyes, we can just imagine it – the music, the freezing January weather, the people, the colour and there, in the centre of it all, Peter the Great.

Peter would certainly have been buried in an English-designed coffin, perhaps even one he had made himself. He is interred in the Cathedral of St Peter and St Paul Fortress in St Petersburg, the city he had made so great when he opened Russia up to the West. There are many memorials to Peter, the most famous perhaps being the Bronze Horseman in St Petersburgh. Peter's tomb is, for many, a sacred place, and many flowers are placed there still. To be remembered well over 200 years later shows the incredible power of this man.

And where did I come into all this? My task was to recreate a coffin, handmade as described above, for an exhibition in Deptford of Peter the Great's life and work. Albin's had previously produced, in the same way, hand-made coffins for royalty so we knew what was required. Terry Card, a wonderful fellow who had worked with us for many years, undertook, with our help, to build the coffin in different open sections for the exhibition. He made a fine job of it, just in time for the opening by Prince Michael of Kent. Albin's provided two limousines for the Prince and his entourage, and he seemed impressed; we spent at least 10 minutes in conversation discussing the coffin and Albin's itself. It was a very rewarding occasion. The coffin made such an impact that it was later exhibited at the Greenwich Maritime Museum – Terry especially was extremely proud. And we were honoured to be helping in forging a link between the past and present.

The right place at the right time: Winston Spencer Churchill (1874–1965)

If such a thing as reincarnation does exist, as many well-respected people believe it does, what would you want to come back as? As a father, it might be fun to come back as your son's son so you can get your own back (although I must say that I'm one of the lucky fathers as being Simon and Jonathan's dad has been a true – if a little wearing – gift!). Some people just seem to be destined to be born when they are needed, as if they were somehow sent to lead us. Just such a man was politician Winston Churchill, a man of his time who might not have fitted into any other, the man who led the United Kingdom through the Second World War to victory. Such was the British debt to this great man that Queen Elizabeth decreed that his final departure was to be a state funeral, one that was to be remembered for all time, the first for a so-called 'commoner' since that of the Duke of Wellington in 1852.

It was 1965, and I was 14 years of age, enjoying school, football and playing trombone in the school brass band. I was looking forward to the World Cup that was to be played in England the following year, swapping cards of the mascot World Cup Willie with all my mates. The nation was then shocked to learn of the death of the Right

Honourable Sir Winston Churchill, which happened at
8 a.m. on 24th January 1965, the seventieth anniversary of
the death of Churchill's father. The following statement
was read by Harold Wilson, then Prime Minister, at 8.55
a.m.: 'It is with great regret that I have heard of the death
of Sir Winston Churchill. He will be mourned all over the
world by all that owe so much to him. He is now at peace
after a life in which he created history and which will be
remembered as long as history is read. Our thoughts and
sympathy are with his family.'

I knew of Winston Churchill through my family.
Bermondsey was heavily bombed during the war, and the
'Churchill spirit' was alive and well there. Even into the
1960s, the view 'We was all one' lived on. And a people
undivided are, as history proves, a formidable foe. Churchill
of course banked on just that kind of reaction to his
leadership; it was the key to his success in guiding the
nation.

A great influence on my youth at the time was Ralph
Reader, my music teacher and form master. He was a
wonderful musician who really cared about us kids and
took time to pass on his wide knowledge of music, English
and history, always with a little fun added. It was Mr
Reader who opened my eyes to the importance of state
occasions such as Churchill's funeral. He played for us
some of the historical mourning music that would be played
at the funeral, and, as a tribute, our brass band was to
learn Handel's moving and inspiring *Death March*. He
even asked the whole class if we would like to go with him
to Tower Bridge to watch Churchill leave by boat from the
pier.

At Albin's, there was much speculation about the funeral.

What would the coffin be like? How heavy would it be? Who would carry it? Would Kenyons, the Royal funeral directors, have the responsibility for organising the proceedings? Indeed, Kenyons were instantly ready to respond. The body of Sir Winston Churchill was removed quietly and prepared, to be embalmed and dressed for lying in state by Desmond Henley. Desmond, who performed this task with admirable ability, conducted himself with discretion and honour over this case and remains to this day very proud of this work. Embalming was not common at this time, and the Churchill family were indeed originally very sceptical of the idea.

The coffin had already been prepared – a solid oak Windsor coffin with an oak shell and lead case, lined and hermetically sealed. In accordance with the Queen's wishes, the coffin containing the body of Sir Winston Churchill was, on 27th January, removed to the Great Hall of Westminster, to lie in state for three days. During this time, over 350,000 citizens came to pay their last respects. Despite the cold, damp, grey weather – the sort of weather that Americans seem to imagine is typical of London – people were not discouraged from queuing for up to five hours.

Churchill himself, never without humour, had been fully aware of the plans for his own funeral, which he named 'Operation Hope Not'. The coffins for all royal and state funerals are made and stored well in advance, and there were many rehearsals for Churchill's funeral, mostly at night and also governed by the tides, so that every step could be paced and every part of the journey timed to perfection. Kenyon's supplied a coffin for rehearsals, loaded with sand bags to the correct weight, and the bearers were trained for hours on end to move their feet properly in order to minimise the movement of the coffin. Were Churchill to die overseas, provision had also already been made to return his body to his beloved England.

So, after all this planning and preparation, at 9.35 a.m. on Saturday 30th January, the bearer party of Grenadier Guards removed the coffin from the catafalque in Westminster Hall on a gun carriage drawn by a gun crew of naval ratings, a carriage steeped in history as it had carried the coffins of Queen Victoria and Kings Edward VII, George V and George VI. The bearer party had been hand picked by Regimental Sergeant Major Randal and represented NCOs and men from the battalion. The main party consisted of ten men – one officer, one warrant officer and eight 'other ranks'. Four extra men (to help carry the coffin up and down the cathedral steps and to distribute the bearskins) and a reserve brought the total to fifteen.

The guns of the Royal Horse Artillery blazed from St James Park on the minute, and guards of honour lined the steps of St Paul's Cathedral to await the arrival of the carriage. The carriage moved at sixty-five paces per minute and, exactly on time, arrived at St Paul's at 10.58. At 10.59, the coffin was carried up the steps of St Paul's, reaching the central aisle of the Church at exactly 11.00 a.m. With the Queen, the Royal Family, Churchill's family and the invited dignitaries all in place, the service began. It included many stirring hymns, as well as prayers read by the Dean and the Archbishop of Canterbury. Fittingly, the National Anthem was sung and the Last Post sounded, before the procession moved from St Paul's to Tower Hill. Here, 90 guns were fired, one for each year of Churchill's life, from the saluting battery at the Tower of London.

And that is where I was too, standing in the cold just along from Courages Brewery on the south side of Tower Bridge with the rest of my class. We had arrived there at around 10 o'clock, the ever-prepared Mr Reader having brought with him four thermos flasks of hot chocolate. After a wait of many hours, we could clearly see, across the river, as fate would have it at full tide just at the right time, the coffin being placed on the *Havengore* launch to the sound of the piping party. A 17-gun salute sounded as the launch moved gently off in a wave of great emotion. The signals were to mark the end of the state funeral and the start of the private family ceremony, but in truth they signalled more than this, indicating instead the end of an era. The cranes on the wharf where we were standing bowed like monsters in a fitting final tribute. Even at 14, the sight made the hairs on the back of my neck stand up.

As I looked on, I could see the guards of honour, the Royal Marines, the Yeoman Wardens of the Tower, and the pipers playing laments. Navy, airforce, army and civilian police were flooding the bank in their striking uniforms. Above roared a fly-past by planes from the Royal Airforce. Churchill's family, riding in two launches, followed the *Havengore* to the pier at the Festival Hall. By now, I could not see any more, so I rushed to the old funeral shop on the Jamaica Road, where we lived, to join Mum and Dad watching the event on television.

Here I saw the coffin being taken by motor hearse from the Festival Pier to Waterloo Station, where a further guard of honour and bearer party from the Irish Hussars placed the coffin on to the train. A Battle of Britain class locomotive named *Winston Churchill* drew the funeral train of Pullman coaches from Waterloo to Long Handborough in Oxfordshire, where Churchill was buried privately in the Church of St Martin's at Bladon next to his mother and father. He had orginally wished to be cremated, his ashes to be scattered at his home, Chartwell, but he changed his Will in 1959. On his grave, there were only two wreaths, one from Churchill's wife with the message 'To my darling Winston, Clemmie' and one that read 'From the Nation and Commonwealth. In grateful remembrance. Elizabeth R.'

As I watched the black and white picture (this was, if you remember, at the time when *Match of the Day* was on BBC2 every Saturday evening but nobody had BBC2 anyway), I could only think of how wonderful the experience had been. It perhaps instilled in me a drive to achieve this level of perfection for everyone I would meet in my work. When I walk in front of a funeral, those memories still sometimes flash through my mind, filling me with pride and leaving me in no doubt about my vocation.

I was full of admiration for Kenyon's and thought then that they must be the best in the world. Little did I imagine that I would one day be part owner and chairman of the international division of Kenyon's, called Kenyon Air Transportation and now renamed Kenyon Christopher Henley Ltd. It's funny how things link up in life. Christopher Henley is the son of the man who embalmed Sir Winston Churchill, a fine funeral director in his own right and part-owner and chief executive of the company. Another instance of events feeling as if they are just meant to happen.

But some things are definitely not meant to be: the hearse that carried Sir Winston strangely crossed my path again later on. The hearse was a 1964 Van Den Plas Austin

Princess, a beautiful purpose-made funeral vehicle. In the late 1980s, I was looking for what we call a bier, in effect a deck that goes in the back of a vehicle to put the coffin on. Seeing that a colleague of mine was advertising such a bier, I booked a visit to see it. It was just what I wanted so I purchased it without delay. When the deal was done, the funeral director said to me, 'Hey Barry, while you're here have a look at this.' He pulled back a dark sheet to reveal, in front of my very eyes, the hearse that had taken Churchill on his final departure, still in good condition after all those years. My memories flooded back – the very hearse I had admired so much on that cold afternoon as I watched on our black and white television with Mum and Dad. 'It's for sale, Barry', he said, '£2500; what do you think?' My mouth fell open. A Princess hearse in good condition would at that time sell for about £500 and I really did not have that kind of extra money to spend, much as I would dearly have loved to as I adore funeral antiquities. I later saw that the hearse had been sold again, this time for £50,000. 'What an idiot you are, Barry,' I thought. 'You should have followed your heart, mate, not your head.'

But then it got worse. In the late 1990s, the hearse was auctioned off to an American for (I can hardly bring myself to tell you) £3,000,000! The owner, an antique dealer in Scotland, said, 'It was in good order and only sold for so much because it started on the button.' Who's he kidding? But I doubt I would ever have made any money even if I had bought it – I'm sure I would not have been able to part with a hearse that had once carried such an exceptional occupant.

4

...And not so famous

If I stand by my belief that everyone who dies is the most important person in the world for a moment, there really is no such thing as a not-so-famous final departure. In death, we are all equal. Take, for example, the five funerals completed by the Memphis Funeral Home while Elvis Presley was awaiting his turn. None of these people were famous in life, but in death they were in every way equally as important. These funerals were completed to perfection even with the pressure of such a famous client waiting. That is exactly how a professional funeral director goes about his or her business: no matter how large or how small, the service must be conducted with the same degree of care and attention. And just like those in the public eye, individuals and families can have very unusual requests.

We recently received a call from a private clinic that was about to undertake a leg amputation for a Muslim gentleman. They wanted us to collect the leg at about 11 that evening and keep it in our deep freeze while the family decided what to do next. In the Islamic religion, they explained, it is important to meet God complete. As all Muslim people are buried (rather than cremated), the leg had to be buried, to be reunited with the rest of the body when the man himself finally died. The problem was, where would he eventually be buried – here or in his place of birth? It took 10 days before the decision was made to bury the leg in Brookwood Cemetery just outside Woking in Surrey. But it is important to respect people's wishes, even if ascertaining them takes some time.

Just as the human team at Albin's aim to treat everyone the same, so too do our animal colleagues. Our horses, Fred and George, are of course not machines to be turned on and off at will, although some drivers seem to think that they have power-assisted brakes and can stop on a sixpence. But what the horse can do really well is embarrass you with its bladder and bowel movements, and sitting on top of a horse-drawn hearse can become quite an occupational hazard. You can be trotting along, no problem, and then the tail will lift and you do not know whether to jump off, sit still or put your hands up and submit. First comes an unpleasant puff of air, then a huge bowel movement and, if you are really unlucky, a violent trump with afterburn that smothers your clean shoes and trousers with manure.

On one particular occasion at Camberwell New Cemetery in South London, Fred and George really made their presence felt. We arrived at the cemetery and carried the deceased to the graveside, the family gathering round in complete quiet. There was no movement; even the day itself was still in every way. Then, almost to order, George opened his rear legs and began to relieve himself. This was a cue for Fred to do the same – in floods. No one moved, all trying to ignore the event, but then just as the coffin was lowered and the minister began the final committal, so Fred and George began to produce enough gas and manure for a whole garden full of roses. Dean, our conductor, could not believe his (dreadful) luck – a solo would have been bad enough but here was a duet, as loud as could be, just like thunder. The horseman, Nick, sat motionless, not even a little smile on his lips. The family burst into spontaneous laughter, unable to control themselves any longer, the laughter, as it often is, being a mixture of joy and tears. The minister took up divine intervention and Dean apologised. But the son said, 'My Dad would have loved this; what a way to say goodbye!', and nature helped just for a moment to ease the pain. Fred and George have no way of knowing when to show what we see as respect and made this a departure to remember. Even so, no more prunes for them!

An example of another person who was not famous in life, but whose death in this case reflected an impact on the whole world, was one of the victims of the World Trade Center terrorist attack on 11th September 2001. The company Kenyon Christopher Henley, of which I am chairman and part owner, had been given the task of repatriating the recovered remains of this person, whom I will call John, one year on from that fateful day when the Twin Towers in New York were destroyed.

After such an inferno, there were only limited remains, but DNA testing and dental records ensured that people could be identified correctly. John could have fitted into a small box but, like any other deceased person, was returned in a respectful traditional American casket, which arrived on the morning flight from New York and was cleared by our import team. Time was precious because the funeral had been arranged in the Midlands for the next day, but John first had to be inspected by the coroner in West London, who would then prepare the documentation. With all such repatriations, it is a requirement to notify the coroner and obtain clearance so that a funeral can take place. Thanks to the efficiency of the coroner, this was completed by lunchtime, and the final part of John's long journey was underway. Just before the registrar's office closed for the day, the last necessary item of documentation, the Liability, was completed, and John was at last returned to his family so that they could say goodbye properly.

Every effort is made to collect the remains of those who are killed in such tragedies, but this is not always possible. Indeed, many of the victims of the World Trade Center disaster could not be recovered, and the same is often true for those killed in air crashes and accidents over deep oceans. However, the major incidents in which I have been involved have been very well organised, and the experts aim to gather not just the remains, but also, wherever possible, other items. Clothes will be found, cleaned, folded and packed for return. Similarly, jewellery will be logged, repaired, cleaned and given back to the family. Major incident teams consist of doctors, pathologists, counsellors, dentists, crash experts, security personnel, the police, embalmers and of course experienced funeral directors. These groups, with their wide range of equipment, are always ready to assist at a moment's notice, as we have seen in such incidents as the Lockerbie aircrash in December 1988 and the Moorgate tube train crash in London in 1975. These people, like those who die in these tragedies, are not famous, but they work tirelessly to grant to many people their right to be laid to rest with dignity.

Sometimes, the famous and not-so-famous share the spotlight. In June 2001, we were asked to undertake the final departure of a Scandinavian gentleman, a renowned and well-respected producer and writer. The family were very precise and knew exactly what they wanted. A double 'slot' was booked at one of London's most prominent crematoriums, and we were put on alert that there would be over 250 people attending. The service was planned, flowers prepared, service sheets and memorial cards printed. One of our attendance books was prepared for the guests to sign. We arrived with plenty of time to spare and began to set up the required music. When the guests began to arrive, I saw some of the most famous stars of television, radio, cinema and of course theatre that I had ever witnessed at an Albin funeral. But I had very little time to stare as I had practical details to attend to.

When there are more people than seats, it is important to try to get guests into position before the coffin is carried in so that you can ask those who have managed to get seats to stand, as a mark of respect, as the deceased enters. Experience and good organisational ability are invaluable at such a large funeral. You have to make sure that those who have to stand through the service are able-bodied, that they are not blocking the view of those who are seated and that everyone can see and hear clearly. If you manage to achieve that with so many people, you have done well! In this case, there was the added factor of dealing with stars such as Pierce Brosnan, Sheila Hancock, Ian McShane and Warren Mitchell, all out of their usual environment and looking for guidance. People in this position can even be a little embarrassed and not want to be near the front, even though they are, in their own field, 'the guvnors', as we would say in South London. But a funeral director never knows what he or she will encounter next.

Many of the guests spoke at this very moving service. The music was uplifting and the whole service an eye-opener for me: this man had lead an inspiring life but had always been in the shadows, unlike the stars he had written for and produced. To the world he was not famous, but he had spent his life making other people famous. Without knowing it, he touched my life and left a final memory of his achievements. As I collected the cards from the flowers, so that I could return them to the family, I could not help noticing how many of them shared the simple words 'Thank you'. A true tribute.

It does us good from time to time to remember that people like this, people who have made a huge contribution to the world we live in yet are around us unrecognised and unheralded. This was brought home to me at a funeral we conducted a few years ago at a Catholic church in Eltham, South London. Father Richard Plunkett, a wonderful priest who has been a dear friend of mine since I was 17, was saying Mass for a man in his late 70s called Tom. The deceased had been taken into church at 7.30 on the evening before the Mass, as is tradition in this part of London, and the church was now about half full. Tom's family – his sons, daughters and grandchildren – all took an active part in the service, his wife having died some years earlier.

As Father Richard began to give the eulogy, it became clear that Tom was no ordinary man. He had been a very talented engineer and inventor who had worked all over the world, being responsible for many of the small, yet important, inventions that technicians now take for granted. But it was not until the son spoke that I truly began to realise how famous Tom should have been. His should have been a name taught to children in school history lessons as Tom was one of the men who had invented and tested the ejector seat. Whatever his direct responsibility in that project, it is clear that he helped to save thousands of pilots from certain death, and how many of us could say a fraction as much of ourselves?

The Mass concluded, we proceeded to the cemetery for the blessing of the grave and final committal. As we lowered the coffin into the ground, I had for a moment the irreverent vision of Tom springing from the grave in an ejector seat. When the funeral party were all chatting and enjoying memories over a drink in the local pub, I was amused to hear Father Richard and Tom's son, Jeff, both confessing that the same thought had also crossed their minds. It was a fitting final departure for a man who truly deserved to be famous because of the difference he had made to the world.

Everyday situations and apparently ordinary people like Tom seem somehow to provide some of the most extra-ordinary tales I have heard from the industry around the world about times past and present. Take the case of Jeremy Bentham. This gentleman was one of the founders of London University and, by all reports, not a very pleasant character; he had once suggested that embalmed corpses could be used for decoration, particularly in the garden. In his Will, in 1832, Bentham stipulated that he be publicly dissected in front of his friends, dressed in his finest clothes and mounted in a chair so that he could continue to attend London University board meetings. The remains of his remains, so to speak, have been present at every meeting and are said to be kept sealed in a cupboard in a glass case.

Further back in history, in the late 1500s, there were continuous wars and skirmishes between Japan and Korea, which came to a climax in 1597 when the Japanese invaded Korea in one massive battle that destroyed much of the Korean army. The Japanese Emperor demanded proof of this victory, but what happened next was lost in legend and the passage of time until, in 1983, a tomb containing 20,000 Korean noses was discovered in Japan – the proof that the Japanese Emperor had demanded. One wonders who had the job of removing the noses and why indeed they chose to do this. Perhaps removing the nose was some sort of insult to the Koreans. Christians in earlier times believed, as Muslims do now, that the body has to be complete to meet God, so for them such an act would have been the final blow; was the same true for the Koreans, or was it just a derogatory act? The Japanese interpreter who was at the time explaining this to me was unable to throw any more light on what had happened, but I was glad to be told that there was a happy ending to this strange but true tale as the noses were finally returned to Korea, where a special ceremony was held to honour them.

A bit less astonishing was the incident of a nine-year-old boy who was, ironically, killed on a school field trip to a cemetery in Ohio, US. On investigating the death, the coroner said that the boy had jumped on the five-foot tall headstone, grabbing it as he did so, the stone then toppling onto the boy and crushing him. Many UK cemeteries now place yellow bags over loose memorials, condemning them to repair or removal.

Some people themselves become famous by not managing

to shuffle off their mortal coil. This happened to Frenchman Angelo Hays, whose life was changed for ever when he 'died' in 1937. Hays was duly buried (thank goodness he was not cremated) but was later, for some reason, dug up and revived, remaining a celebrity until his true final departure many years later.

Anne McCall, commemorated in a graveyard in County Armagh, Northern Ireland, is another of the elite of this world who have been able to have a practice run at dying. Anne was just 21 years of age, married and of a happy disposition, when she appeared to have some kind of heart attack and was declared dead. She was buried the same day, but that night her grave was visited by grave-robbers, who opened up her coffin in their search for valuable jewellery. Spotting Anne's wedding ring, they brutally began to cut off her finger, but these ruthless villains were about to have the shock of their lives as blood flowed from her cut finger. The act must have caused Anne to recover and stir in her coffin, sending the two men fleeing in panic. It is said that Anne calmly rose from her grave and went home to her husband – and what a shock that must have been for him too! Anne eventually had her final departure 60 years later, this time to rest in peace.

History has always labelled such grave-robbers – of which there are sadly still a few today – and body-snatchers as the lowest of the low, depriving so many of their final rest and dignity. Often once referred to as 'resurrectionists', 'body-snatchers' were only interested in removing the body, grave-robbers intending to rob the dead. How desperate must these criminals have been to carry out such acts.

The problem was largely created by the passing of the Anatomy Act of 1800, which made it compulsory for members of the medical profession to have worked on human corpses before they were let loose on the living. The two most infamous body-snatchers were undoubtedly Burke and Hare, expert Irish labourers who had begun their working life digging the Union Canal. In their new career, however, they went further than your common body-snatcher, forming a deadly partnership to murder their drinking pals and sell the bodies fresh, if somewhat pickled from the strong drink, to Dr Knox of Edinburgh and his anatomy dissecting rooms. A second government Bill in 1830, however, legalised and regulated anatomy schools so body-snatching was brought to an end. Were the anatomy schools to blame for demanding and accepting bodies without question? It must have been a difficult situation as there were so many students needing to understand the workings of the anatomy and an endless demand for bodies, the legally given bodies of paupers and hung murderers being not nearly enough.

Professional body-snatchers were cunning animals with a cunning plan. Under cover of darkness and having already spotted the new, fresh graves, they would carefully cut open the head of the grave to expose the coffin lid. Smashing this would enable them to pull the body up through the small head opening. The body-snatchers were then able to replace the soil and leave, often with no trace of what they had done. The bodies would be hidden in barrels or boxes to be sent to the dissecting rooms of the trainee doctors.

The following letter was printed in a Belfast Parish Newsletter on 28th January 1824 after the grave of a child was opened in a Belfast cemetery. The corpse was obviously of no use as it was not fresh so the desecrators left the corpse, coffin and all the mess and fled. The letter reads:

A reward of fifty pounds is offered by the Committee of the Belfast Charitable Society to any person who shall, within six weeks, give information to the Steward against and prosecute, to conviction, the person or persons guilty of the atrocious offence of entering the burying ground behind the poorhouse on Monday night 12th last and raising an infant coffin, several years interred it remained unopened on the ground.

To protect their loved ones, some people designed a form of cage to be placed over the grave, some of which can still be seen today. They were sold as coffin guards and were very successful in preventing body-snatchers from carrying out their dirty deeds. Wealthy grave-owners would employ grave-watchmen, whereas other less wealthy individuals took it in turn to sit night after night to protect the grave.

Sometimes mortuaries were the scene of a snatch, or funerals were attacked and the bodies stolen. Funeral directors wielded truncheons to protect against such attacks, and even today bearers walk alongside the hearse, and the conductor, in front, often carries a large stick to ward off evil spirits – as well as cars and bikes in our ever-changing modern world. The undertaker in those days was usually a trustworthy man, but some unscrupulous individuals would sell the bodies and fill the coffin with heavy stones or earth before burying it. As the average pay for a skilled labourer was about £2 a week, and that for the unskilled £1.50, earning 'double bubble' by selling a body – for the enormous sum of about £14 – was very tempting, and a skilled body-snatcher could scrounge a couple a night.

Unfortunately, the punishment does not always fit the crime. Body-snatching was judged to be a 'misdemeanour', attracting only minimal punishment, as long as the body-snatcher took only the body. If, however, he took anything off the body – clothes or jewellery, for example – the crime became theft and he would receive a heavy punishment because he was then a grave-robber. Thomas Vaughnan, a renowned body-snatcher, and his equally bad wife, were caught and tried for grave-robbing as they had, for some strange reason, stolen a petticoat off a body, despite knowing the punishment. They were sentenced to transportation to Tasmania and hard labour, whereas two other criminals found guilty at the same trial of body-snatching received only the ridiculous sentence of two weeks' imprisonment with hard labour.

Luckily, I have had only minimal experience of grave-robbery. About 20 years ago, I was called to a local crypt under a large church, which had been violated. On our arrival, we found two oak coffins and lead cases that had been broken open to expose the deceased within them. It was a very eerie moment to see two people who had died over a hundred years before. One, a woman aged 32 years at the time of her death, still had auburn hair, and, although her skin was wrinkled like a prune, her features were sharp and haunting. Even now, I can clearly see her lying there in her white burial shroud. The gentleman from the other coffin had a large ginger beard and had been aged 61 years when he died. In life, one had been quite famous, the other unknown, but at that moment they shared the same hideous fate, which truly saddened me.

My second exposure to this awful crime occurred when
a mortician was caught stealing money, jewellery and
personal effects from the dead, a very unusual situation as
morticians are, as a group, fine professionals and completely
trustworthy. This man, however, had been quite mad. He
lived on site and could often be found in shorts, a vest and
a First World War German helmet when we took in night
calls for an autopsy. He was indeed the talk of the mortuary.
The man eventually gave himself away when he boasted of
his deed in the local pub in front of a person who had
police connections. He was then found guilty of robbery
and was sentenced to something like five years in prison.
When they searched his home, the police found clothes,
rings, watches, credit cards, hundreds of cigarette packets,
all of different brands, and ladies' high-heeled shoes, a
bizarre collection from the poor people he was responsible
for on their last journey.

Thank goodness that individuals like this are the
exception rather than the rule in the funeral business. But
that is not to say that some of the characters involved are
not just a bit eccentric or the happenings surrounding
them somewhat comical. Mr A. Dyer (I think perhaps a
distant relative), like me a funeral director in East London,
albeit back in the 1920s, ran a small number of funeral
shops and also a masonry yard. His father had, I believe,
begun the business in the late 1800s. Mr Dyer was involved
in the business and was also an officer in the First World
War, returning afterwards to follow in his father's footsteps
as an undertaker. He was well known for his trips to the
US, from where he brought back many new ideas. One of
these was 'sanitation', a form of embalming preservation
that became his trademark. He would always explain the

process to his customers, telling them that if sanitation were undertaken, they could rest assured that the bodies of their loved ones would be kept in good condition when they were laid out at home (a tradition from those days that is seen far less today). It was common practice in those days for undertakers to assist each other with hearses and bearers. The undertaking firm of Hitchcock's, now, I am proud to say, owned by Albin's, was well renowned for its wonderful hearses. As Mr Dyer was very friendly with Mr Hitchcock, he would often hire one of his hearses for a funeral or laying at rest at home. On this occasion (as Russell, Mr Hitchcock's nephew, explained to me), the hire was for a hearse and men to take a gentleman to his home, where his wife and family were waiting to say goodbye.

Spending the last few days with a body was very important to most families so Mr Hitchcock duly obliged and took the gentleman home, where he was laid out. Laying out usually took place in the front room; trestles would be placed on a special rug, and the coffin would be placed on these trestles, always foot to the door so that the deceased would leave home feet first, as he did during life. Candlesticks were arranged so that an altar could be made up for family prayers. If the family were Roman Catholic, a crucifix was placed in the centre of the altar, and the priest would visit the home to bless the body and recite the rosary with the relatives. All the mirrors were covered to prevent reflections, and the windows were draped with a clean white sheet so that sunlight could not enter and make shadows. A large, and rather frightening, memorial card, often portraying a Rock of Ages or an angel, would be placed in the window, bearing the person's details and the date and time of the funeral so that no one would have to ask. The neighbours would then take round a subscription list to collect money to help pay for the funeral or for a few flowers out of respect, not, as originally required, to blot out the stench of putrefaction. Everybody's name would go on the list, as would the amount they pledged; if, unthinkably, the sum pledged was not paid, a big 'X' would be placed by the name of that person – a real stigma. The final part of the laying to rest at home was to check that all windows were closed and that the room was as cold as possible. A net pall was then placed over the coffin, and a lace face cloth to keep flies off the deceased's face.

On this occasion, Mr Hitchcock had been well briefed by Mr Dyer and reminded to tell the family not to worry as the body was 'sanitised'. Mr Hitchcock called the family in to pay their respects. Taking the wife quietly aside so that she could see her husband first, he proclaimed to her that her husband looked very peaceful and at rest, leaving her, so the story goes, very tearful but very content. The room was now full when Mr Hitchcock and his staff, ready to leave, remembered Mr Dyer's instructions. Not really knowing what he was talking about but wishing to follow Mr Dyer's wishes to the last letter, Mr Hitchcock turned and called for the attention of all present, saying in a wonderful cockney accent 'All 'ere present, could I please 'ave your eyes and ears for one moment. Mr Dyer asks that you don't worry about the continued good 'ealth of the body whilst the deceased is lying stately at home because the body 'as been . . .'. At this point, his mind went completely blank and, groping for the right word, he continued, 'the body 'as been sterilised.' You can just imagine the total confusion on the family's faces! Mind you, they probably would not have known what sanitisation was in any case. But the staff knew the difference and could hardly contain themselves. Mr Hitchcock, ever the professional, simply continued with 'Anyway, you've got no worries; goodbye to one and all', turned and took his leave.

Having recently gone through some of the old family paperwork, Russell recently showed me a book reflecting death in the late 1800s. The fascinating document was full of records and a number of accounts of those who had either died at home or been laid out there, a very interesting record. In some cases, bodies were, for one reason or another, left unattended for weeks in a corner. Imagine the smell, the flies, the maggots; it must have been dreadful. Just think – people had to cook, eat and sleep in the same room. One account told of a woman who had lost her husband, reportedly to a fever (a common cause of death in those days), the body being left to rest at home in a coffin. The wife continued to kiss his body and, needless to say, within a week she had caught a fever and followed her husband to their Maker. The conditions, lack of hygiene and deprivation of former times must have contributed to the spread of disease; thank goodness things are so different today.

But just like today, 90 per cent of the funerals of yesteryear were those of ordinary people. In those days, however, the undertaker would operate a very class-conscious system so that people could see the status of the deceased, the class of the funeral being depicted by the ribbon worn around the conductor's hat. Bottom of the pile – for ordinary folks – would be cotton, with crêpe for the businessperson or costermonger. Finally, for top-class funerals, conductors would wear a silk ribbon around their hat. A 'silk' funeral had the best of everything, and the world was to know all about it.

I love tradition, but I am very glad to say that this particular one has been discarded. For me, every funeral conducted, however small or large, however simple or grand, holds the same importance, whether you are rich or poor, notorious or ordinary. We can't all be famous, but we are all definitely special.

5
Amazing embalmings

Since time immemorial, man has tried to preserve the dead. Indeed, embalming is probably one of the world's oldest professions. Even in the Bible (Genesis 50:3), it says, 'Joseph commanded the Physicians to embalm his Father and the Physicians embalmed Israel.' Over many thousands of years, man has found simple ways to successfully, and sometimes unsuccessfully, preserve the dead, techniques known as sanitation, mummification, hygienic treatment or embalming, albeit unlike the modern scientific embalming process we use today. Strictly speaking, any procedure that restricts decomposition is a form of preservation and can therefore be described as a form of embalming, but what really is embalming, and how can we understand it in simple modern terms?

Like certain other medically related procedures, scientific embalming involves minor surgical techniques. In a specialised room resembling a hospital operating theatre, well-trained embalming operators perform, very professionally, a procedure resembling a kind of blood transfusion or dialysis. Using surgical instruments and wearing the appropriate protective clothing, they replace the blood and body fluids with preservatives and disinfectant solutions, at the same time releasing the body's gases and slowing the natural process of decomposition. Embalming can remove the harsh physical effects of a long illness or accident and often restores a natural appearance. I have always felt that embalming is as much for the living as the dead as it allows people to say goodbye with assurance and in their own time. Embalming can take place only after the death has been legally recorded, but the sooner it is carried out, the better the results. As the results are hygienic as well, the procedure benefits everyone.

In the US, each state has its own requirements, but embalmers are licensed and must be fully qualified in accordance with the state laws. In the UK, the excellent British Institute of Embalming operates very high standards and is extremely professional, also running student courses and exams. This and the National Association of Funeral Directors are to be commended as both lead the way for the industry. Not all embalmers, however, are members of the Institute: some have learnt the skill in the family business and never joined; others have been privately taught or have studied abroad in Europe or the US.

I have always had an interest in embalming; the very word echoes intrigue and mystery. Although I have attended courses, lectures, conventions, crash scenes, murder scenes and disasters the world over and experienced so much related to death and embalming, I still consider myself to be merely a beginner in the field. Over the years, some incidents of embalming have particularly intrigued me. The two I am going to describe here are those of Eva Peron and Vladimir Lenin.

Eva Peron (1919–1952)

Before I was even two years old, the beautiful stunning blonde Eva Peron (born Eva Duarte) had already reached great heights of fame and died a legend on 26th July 1952, aged 33 years. To the poor, Eva was a saint, a distributor of wealth, the saviour of Argentina. To the wealthy, she was a despicable, ruthless woman without class. To me, she seems to be someone just very confused in life but passionately committed to her people.

Eva was born without position, an illegitimate child stigmatised by society, who fought with determination to become a somebody. She was working as an actress when she had the good fortune to meet General Juan Peron, the future President of Argentina, which changed her life for ever. Eva gained respect, wealth and power, and won the hearts of the people like no leader had done before. She gained many supporters and many enemies, none greater than the cancer that eventually overtook her. Despite a valiant fight, she could not control it as she did the rest of her life. It was reported, perhaps to create some sort of stigma as this was said to be the hour of her marriage to Peron, that she died at 8.25 p.m. From the moment of her last words to her sister, Elisa – 'Eva se va' (Eva is leaving) – until the fall of the Peron regime, the radio news was stopped nightly at 8.25 to remind people that this was the time at which Eva Peron had, as Juan Peron described it, entered immortality. At 8.25 p.m., that fateful hour when

Argentina mourned the loss of an ordinary woman who destiny had somehow shaped into the portrayal of greatness, a portrayal under which still lay that simple lovely woman who felt passionately for the people, a responsibility too heavy for anyone.

The show of grief that followed Eva's death was so grand and spectacular that it is beyond belief. Her followers were ordered to wear black ties and armbands. Flags flew at half-mast and were covered in black, as were the lampposts in every city. All businesses except florists were ordered to close for three days. Quietly inside the privacy of Casa Rosada, the presidential palace, the very famous pathologist Dr Pedro Ara was ready to face the challenge of a lifetime as he prepared to embalm Eva Peron.

Dr Ara had spent much of his life perfecting his unique technique to preserve the dead for, as he would put it, an indefinite period of time. He would first replace the blood with neat alcohol and then replace the alcohol with glycerine. He would heat the fluid to a high temperature, the theory being that the alcohol would dehydrate the tissue and the glycerine would replace the water, saturating the tissue and giving a life-like look to the body. This also had good preservative powers and would fully protect the body, organs and tissue. Only two points – one in the neck, the other in the foot – were used for this form of embalming, these two small but precise surgical cuts being sufficient to inject and remove the fluids. Dr Ara's work on Eva Peron was slow and painstaking, he and his assistant working all through the night until the late morning. His own words were, 'The body of Eva Peron is now definitely incorruptible.'

Dr Ara used to compare notes with Des Henley of

Kenyon's, the man who embalmed Sir Winston Churchill, and, when I was a young man, Des would often show me these fascinating letters.

In the descriptions Dr Ara wrote to Des, he described, in some detail, the embalming process and treatment of the skin. I can still remember parts of it now. He talked about using lanolin and wax on Eva's beautiful blonde hair, and about how, with the help of his assistants, he had taken each strand and treated it one piece at a time. He spoke of her gentle skin and how he massaged in special lanolin-based cream.

With the body embalmed, it was time to call in other specialists to complete the final touches. This was to be Eva's final farewell appearance, but little did they know what was in store and how there would be many turns before Eva would take her final bow. Her personal dressmaker had worked through the night to fashion a unique burial gown, an ivory-coloured tunic, for her last journey. Her personal hairdresser, who had styled her hair daily for her entire adult life, applied a little extra colour and then fashioned her tresses into her trademark chignon for the last time. Then came her manicurist, who cleaned her nails and painted them, as Eva herself had instructed, with a pale colour instead of the crimson colour she loved to wear, which was thought to be too striking in death. Dr Ara made a final inspection, and the order was given for the undertakers to bring the beautiful bronze coffin to the Casa Rosada. The one-off coffin, specially chosen by Eva, who missed no detail in either her life or her death, was tailormade by Lynch Metalworking of Connecticut, US, at a cost of $30,000. In the centre, was an inch-thick crystal cover, hermetically sealed but allowing those who wished to pay their last respects to view Eva through the glass.

In Eva's hands was placed a mother of pearl rosary with silver clasps, very special to her in her life as a Roman Catholic and given to her in person by Pope Pius XII. The last touch to the preparation for state viewing was the blue and white Argentinian flag, which was draped over the now-sealed coffin. It was moved, with Eva, to the Ministry of Labour Building (the home of the people, you might say) for the lying in state. A Mass was celebrated by the Archbishop of Buenos Aires, Monsignor Manuel Tato, and Eva's personal friend and priest, Father Herman Bentley.

The state viewing lasted an incredible 13 days. It is said that rain fell endlessly for this whole period, some passionate Peronists believing this to be Eva's tears falling from heaven. Over three million people, all weeping, passed her coffin during that time. Some queued for 14 hours in the rain for the privilege; some stopped and embraced the casket or kissed the glass. Many fainted, and over four thousand people were treated by nurses and volunteers while queuing. A number of people even died in the furore of the occasion and their passion to see Eva's remains. The flowers from her people piled high in the sky, leaving a mixture of smells as the fresh blooms covered the dying ones many feet below. With his great political passion and love, Juan Peron could not let her go so he decided that there would be yet another day's viewing, this time in the Congress Building.

The next morning, a further Mass was celebrated and many fine words said in Eva's favour. The body, the coffin now fully closed and draped with the blue and white flag, was placed on to a gun carriage for the state funeral. At the front of the cortège were union officials, there was mourning music, flowers were thrown from balconies, and the airforce ran flypast after flypast. After about three hours, the carriage arrived at the Labour and Social Welfare Building, temporary accommodation while Eva's tomb was being prepared. Surely this signalled the final stages of her journey? But no – this was only the beginning of her story in death.

Eva was taken to Dr Ara's laboratory, occupying a complete floor in the building, where he cared for her remains and continued his work for over a year. By now, this can only be described as an obsession. In one of his letters to Des, Dr Ara mentioned that he was to be paid over and above his state earnings, a sum in excess of $40,000, but it is unsure whether he ever received such an amount. When Juan Peron was exiled to Spain, it was said that Dr Ara went with the family and lived in a beautiful villa with them there.

But what more could be done to achieve the mummification of Eva? Dr Ara disclosed very little detail of his work in that final year, and he was constantly disturbed in his work. Eva's mother and three sisters visited weekly, and many dignitaries were given permission to do so too, but thousands upon thousands were refused audience with her. Flowers were still laid daily at the foot of the building, but there is no record that Peron ever visited the great love of his life. It is said that Dr Ara used an ancient method of Spanish mummification that would soak the whole circulatory system, the cavities then being packed with a thick, wax-like material and the body finally covered with a waxy layer to create a final seal. In the mid-summer of 1953, Dr Ara's work was at an end, but the mausoleum was still not ready to receive 'Santa Evita', as she had become to her thousands of followers. By now, the Pope had received over 100,000 requests to canonise Eva, but he resisted and refused them all.

When, in 1955, Peron was removed from power in a military coup, the new generals' first move was to remove Eva, and all traces of her, from Argentina to prevent her leading a Peronist revival from the grave. They stole her body from Dr Ara's laboratory and hid it in the back of a lorry that was parked in different places in Buenos Aires and in the army stores. They never seemed to consider destroying her body – were they afraid of her, even in death? – although there are many rumours that her body was abused. At this time, it was even a crime to mention Eva's name in public, and every charity that she had put her name to was closed or renamed. All statues and the mausoleum were destroyed. The Peronists meanwhile demanded to know where Eva's body was, but they were ignored until their voice was finally too strong to push aside. In 1957, with the help of Pope Pius XII, Eva's body was removed to a small part of an Italian cemetery, the Musocco in Milan, although not to be finally at rest but only temporarily buried under the assumed name of Maria Maggi. There she remained until 1971.

Back in Argentina, things were hotting up and the Peronists were gaining strength, calls being made to have Eva returned to her beloved Argentina. As a compromise, the regime agreed to assist in releasing the whereabouts of Eva's body, eventually returning it to Peron in an unmarked vehicle in September 1974 to try to calm Peronist supporters in Argentina. Dr Ara waited anxiously to see his work. Had his recipe for the perfect embalming been a success? Would Eva's remains be nothing but a skeleton? For Dr Ara, a renowned pathologist with a life-long interest in preservation, this would be either his crowning moment or his biggest failure. With great anticipation, he opened the coffin, still in good condition after all those years. What he saw next must have been very emotional for him as there in front of him, perfectly preserved, was Eva. There was a little exterior damage that Dr Ara was easily able to repair, and, ironically, Peron's new wife, Isabel (a dancer and yet another strong, wilful woman), combed and styled Eva's still perfect hair in preparation for her possible return home to Argentina. A new gown was handmade, and Eva was placed in the attic of the Peron's Madrid home.

One year later, Peron returned to Argentina and again became President, this time with Isabel at his side. For a while, Eva's body stayed in the attic of the Madrid villa. Peron did not rule for long as he died in July 1974, leaving Isabel fully in charge (which, ironically, had always been Eva's dream). Isabel ordered Eva's body to be returned, and she lay in state for the second time alongside her former husband at the presidential home in Buenos Aires. Amazingly, Eva's body was on full view and still very beautiful, even after approximately 22 years. Although Peron himself had been dead for only a matter of days, his coffin was sealed and his body was not on view, which must be proof that Dr Ara's skill and method of embalming were of the very highest quality. In my opinion, he is one of the best embalmers of all time.

Two years later, Isabel herself was overthrown. The new President wanted to live at the presidential palace but not with the remains of Eva and Juan so he ordered that they should be both buried in the Duarte family mausoleum in the Cementerio de la Recoleta, Buenos Aires' most prestigious cemetery. Written in Spanish on the tomb are the words 'Don't cry for me Argentina', later echoed by Andrew Lloyd Webber's hit musical *Evita*. Later, in 1998, I found myself, not by chance, in Buenos Aires. This was a wonderful moment. I had studied Eva's life and embalming, I had read Dr Ara's letters to Des, I had seen *Evita*; now I was on the streets where she lived.

It was May and I was about to be appointed as the UK representative of the world association representing the funeral industry: Fédération Internationale des Associations de Thanatologues/International Federation of Thanatologists Association (FIAT/IFTA). Over 200 funeral representatives from 29 countries filled the conference halls at the famous Buenos Aires racecourse. I remember how much like England Buenos Aires seemed; even the weather made me feel at home – wet yet pleasant, early spring-like days. Having attended the meetings and lectures, I could not wait to slip off to visit the government buildings and the de la Recoleta cemetery. I was lucky to have with me my international colleague and travel companion Carole Bearden, who, like me, was fascinated as we toured Buenos Aires.

As we arrived at the cemetery, it was interesting to witness first hand a local funeral. The hearse and cars were a little tacky, but the coffin was very elegant. It was carried into church by its handles, rather than on men's shoulders. The men were all dressed in different coloured suits, Argentinian tradition dictating that the body and the coffin, rather than the accessories or the formalities, are the central part of the funeral. It was drizzling with rain, and the cemetery mausoleums threw shadows on the pathways as the afternoon sun began to set. We walked around the cemetery with a written guide, but the Duarte family mausoleum was not as easy to find as I thought it would be. It was of course locked, and the windows were too grimy to see through clearly, but for me there was a sense of history about the place.

I was standing by the opening of the mausoleum thinking how much I would like to be able to see Dr Ara's great work. All you would have to do would be to open the mausoleum, unseal the coffin and there she would be. But then I thought about the sacredness of the body and how Eva should finally be allowed to rest in peace. There were no flowers left at this particular mausoleum, and no one seemed to mention her name. When I asked about her in the funeral homes I visited in Buenos Aires, they would just shrug their shoulders as if to say, those days have passed. Surely, despite the attempt to eradicate her presence after Peron's regime had been removed for the first time, some things just stick, don't they? It was only a conversation with the Argentinian representative that finally led me to understand Eva's continuing influence in Argentinian politics.

In 1959, it is said that Eva's fingers or hands were stolen and a ransom note for £5,000,000 was received. This must have been the last straw for the authorities and led to drastic action. Eva's journey ended when she was moved from the Duarte mausoleum and placed in a tomb deep under a building in the centre of Buenos Aires, sealed with tons of cement and never again to be revealed. The representative explained that the mausoleum was always being written on, and banners and many flowers were placed there, reflecting Eva's undying influence. The Argentinian military of that time, a very powerful and very determined regime, removed all trace of her body so that she could never be exhumed as a powerful political inspiration to the people.

Thanks to a helpful, English-speaking taxi driver, I found this spot in Buenos Aires. Eva's name, written on a plaque along with some other words in Spanish, is all that is left of this remarkable woman and this amazing period of history. Being covered in tons of concrete is such a sad end. As I looked at the plaque amid a busy street, I confess I felt very emotional. Could Eva now finally be at rest? Maybe one day, thousands of years from now, some archaeologist will even find her body and wonder how it could have survived in such condition. Not only Argentina's greatest legend and one of the world's most talked about women, but surely one of the world's greatest examples of modern embalming.

Vladimir Ilyich Ulyanov – Vladimir Lenin (1870–1924)

When I look back and reflect on my childhood, Saturdays are, without a doubt, right up there as my best ever days. First, up early to get the comics – the *Valiant*, the *Victor* – with their fantastic comic characters: Ted Legs, Tough of the Track and Roy of the Rovers. Then off to the CUM (the Cambridge University Mission, commonly known as Come You Mugs) or the OBC (Oxford and Bermondsey Club, which we called Our Bloody Club), both great Bermondsey boys clubs that we flitted between. Saturday was football day at the clubs. We would all pile onto an old double-decker bus and head off to the Federation of Boys Clubs sports field at Bellingham to play against other clubs.

Back for 1 o'clock to hear the opening tune of *Sports Report* with Eamon Andrews on the radio. He would introduce reports in such places as Molineux, the ground of famous Wolverhampton Wanderers, and Anfield, home to mighty Liverpool FC. It was on one such programme that I first heard of Russia.

Eamon was reporting on a football team about to play in England, I guess in the European Cup. I will never forget their name: nothing dreary like Middlesbrough or Birmingham (not that I have anything against those places!) but, to a kid, cor, a brilliant name. They were called Moscow Dynamos. And, to top it all, they were very good. Mum got the atlas out, and we looked first for Russia and then Moscow. At eight years old, I thought that a football team was more important than a capital city, so I was looking for Moscow Dynamos on the map, but Mum soon put me right. It was then that I first realised how small Great Britain was.

My mother, Mary Angela, was a gentle and very patient lady. She and Dad were my life. I remember she went to the library and got a book about Russia. As I was not a great reader at the time (I only looked at the headlines and the pictures!), she would read bits out to me, and that is where I first heard the name Lenin. There was a picture of his dead body on the centre spread of the book. 'Spooky', I thought, even though I was living at the time in a Chapel of Rest. I rushed down to ask Dad about the picture. Dad looked at this dead man in a glass box, and I remember him smiling and saying, 'That's not him boy, that's a wax model.' 'Really Dad, are you sure?' 'No one really knows, son, but look at him, doesn't he look like a wax model? I'll take you to Madame Tussauds. You can see hundreds of famous wax models there.' True to his word, Dad did take me; I must have been a very morbid child as I remember liking the chamber of horrors best!

From then, I was always interested in Lenin, the body. I guess he was Russia's Roy of the Rovers. In my simple boyhood terms, he always came out on top, a real leader. I have truly never had any real ambition to go to Russia but an '80 seconds that I would remember for the rest of my life' would be perfect. That is how much time you are allowed to spend looking at Lenin's body in the great centre hall of the mausoleum in Red Square, Moscow, where the sarcophagus lies in all its splendour. Armed sentries protect the opening of this historic building, and the queues begin to form well before the daily opening time of 11 a.m. People, I am told, shuffle quietly through the hall. Not a word is heard, only the footsteps of the endless daily queues of visitors.

So who was this man, and why is he preserved here for all to see? A recent poll in Russia, over 10 years after the death of communism, showed that two-thirds of the Russian people have affection for Lenin. That's 131 years after the birth of the man who is clearly recognised as the leader of the Bolsheviks and the father of the communist revolution. There have been strong moves to dispose of his embalmed remains, but the people themselves have greatly opposed this, which has led to one leader after another being too afraid to make such a stand against Lenin and change the venue of his final departure.

Like Eva Peron, Lenin has in some ways become, in his death, a figure of historical power. The powerful embalming techniques and camouflaging used by the Russians to preserve him are still something of a mystery, even today.

Try as I may, I have been unable to get to the bottom of one of Russia's best-kept bits of information; in fact, I understand that this is still considered an official state secret. The best descriptions I have found have been by Llya Zbarsky, the son of the man who headed the 'Lenin Project' (Lenin's embalming), in his 1998 book *In the Shadow of the Mausoleum*, and by Fred Weir, a journalist who wrote a wonderful probing account for *The Independent Magazine*.

Interestingly, Lenin's body was autopsied, and, it would seem, parts were removed. There is even speculation that his brain was taken out and pickled. Zbarsky recorded that the veins and arteries had been removed at autopsy, so conventional scientific embalming could not be carried out. Zbarsky writes that the scientists on the project were forced to use a form of embalming called total immersion. A large vat was made and filled with an unknown formula of preservatives. The remains were then washed with water and different concentrations of alcohol, followed by a solution of potassium acetate. Cuts were made surgically in all parts of the body to enable a better penetration of the solutions, and the remains were immersed in the preservatives for an unstated period.

Amazingly, at the end of every 18 months, on the dot, the remains are removed from the case and taken to a secret area where a fully trained team of undertakers, embalmers and scientists is waiting to rejuvenate the body. The body is reimmersed in the vat for a two-month period, the 12-person team, permanently retained in a department named 'The Kremlin Centre for Biological Structure', then undertaking surgical touch-ups and other 'private confidential treatments'. These days, Lenin has to be completely covered in a wetsuit to prevent his body disintegrating. This 'private and confidential treatment' suggests to me that my Dad was right and there must be a layer of wax over the outer surface of the face. Nevertheless, this is a wonderful show of embalming skills. The remains are then dressed and positioned for a further 18 months. If they ever decided to give Lenin a final end and a state funeral, who would be asked I wonder – would capitalists sit alongside communists in our modern world? Ken Livingstone next to Queen Elizabeth?

A friend of mine once described to me his '80 seconds with Lenin'. 'When you arrive at the mausoleum, it is very daunting, like a blast from the past, before even arriving at the entrance after a two-hour wait. The sharply dressed guards instructed us to be silent throughout our visit (I say instructed because that is exactly how it was), to keep quietly moving and not to loiter at any point (hence the 80 second shuffle). The room where Lenin lies is very dark except for a light that is above his remains. He is dressed in a dark suit, and it all seems very sinister and a little unnerving. Everybody obeys the silence rule, and only the movement of the visitors can be heard. He's been dead since 1924 but he looks very fresh and new, a bit like wax. But I loved every moment, Barry', he concluded.

In the wall behind the Lenin mausoleum, my friend also saw the tomb of a great name from the 1960s, that of Russian cosmonaut, Yuri Gagarin, the first man in space. As a child of the 60s, my friend was as much in awe of that tomb as he was of Lenin's. History seems to be very special when you have lived through it but far more exciting when you wished you had. Lenin might one day be put out of sight, out of reach, but for now he remains in his sarcophagus, in his personal mausoleum, getting regular personal make-overs at a cost of £1,000,000 each year. So far, at today's prices, that could amount to around £70,000,000, probably the highest-priced embalming of all time, but one that Russia seems to regard as worth paying. With that sort of retainer, I would definitely consider becoming 'Albinoffs, undertakers to the Russian leaders'.

My only recent business connection to Russia came in the form of a request for some stylish coffins and caskets. A very enterprising Russian shipping company called at the small factory where we manufacture special coffins and stock many other unique caskets, for example American steel, bronze and copper caskets, Italian hand-crafted 'Last Supper' coffins and hand-painted coffins in many designs. The two representatives, Russian but with a very good understanding of English, were wearing Armani suits, Hugo Boss shoes and smiles to match. When I asked, 'Isn't there a problem with money in Russia; who could possibly afford to buy one of these there?', they just smiled their enigmatic smiles. 'For us is no problem, and we have many customers with plenty of money. Albin, have you ever heard of the Russian Mafia?' In truth, I had not at that time heard of them. 'No', I replied. 'Well, you soon will', they sniggered. 'We will want to purchase 50 coffins and caskets every quarter, and we want a very good price, you understand me?' 'Gurp', I thought to myself but regained my composure: 'As long as it's all above board, correctly invoiced and you pay in advance, there will be no problem, gentlemen.' 'Good. We send lorry next week, we take this one, this one . . .'.

Well, the deal was done, the documents exchanged and the coffins and caskets shipped two weeks later. That was about five years ago, and I have not heard from them since. A while ago, there was a television documentary on the Russian Mafia and the regular killings in that area. I spotted a Last Supper casket in the programme – was it one of ours? I understand though from embalming contacts, that there is a kind of underground embalming movement in Moscow that offers Lenin-type embalming, at very high cost, to the Mafia. Many of the assassinated Mafia leaders receive this treatment, special caskets and idolisation from their followers. It could be said that there is little difference from Lenin here; both were, after all, leaders of one kind or another involved in life and death daily decisions, but how many Mafiosi will survive their embalming for over 76 years? Not many, I'll wager!

6

A nation in mourning

Bereavement is a universal and integral
part of our experience of love.

C. S. Lewis

We recently conducted a local funeral for a family we had
not had the privilege of serving before. It was, for this
brother and sister, the first time that they had undertaken
the responsibility of arranging a funeral, not something
that, in truth, anyone can be prepared for, whatever their
age or the age of the person they have lost. The funeral this
couple arranged with Jackie at the office was for their
mother, Gracie. Gracie was 76 years old when she died
peacefully in hospital. It can be just as difficult, albeit in a
different way, losing your mother at this age as it would be
if she were much younger; after all, this brother and sister
would not have known a day of their lives without her. The
longer you have someone, the harder it can be to lose them,
and every detail becomes important in these situations.

The funeral went ahead just as the couple had wanted, and about a week afterwards, they came to see Jackie with a small gift of chocolates, just to show their appreciation. After spending a little time with Jackie, they came into reception as I was arriving and we talked about Gracie's ashes and how they were going into our cremation cemetery memorial garden at Albin's. As they were about to leave, the son paid us one of the nicest and most unusual compliments I have ever received. He simply said, 'You know Barry, when we arrived at Albins to arrange the funeral for Mum, we were both very stressed and confused. Neither of us had slept much, and we had queued all morning at the hospital and registrars, so, to say the least, we were edgy. We came in to a friendly smile from Joanna, were shown in to Jackie and, by the time we left and got into the car, we looked at each other and both realised that for a while we had forgotten why we were here. Mum had been dead from Friday evening, we got to you Monday afternoon, and in all that time not a moment had passed without Mum's death staring us in the face. It was as we sat in the car that we both knew things would get better. Our time with Jackie proved that. Even though we were talking about Mum, and her funeral, the pain had gone for a while and that was so helpful. Thank you all.' I was a little choked and very proud of their kindness. For these two people, this was the first step to beginning again. You never get over the loss, but you do learn how to go on and adjust. For a time, putting one foot in front of the other and seeing what the next day brings is the best you can do.

When we lose someone so close, the pain is expected and, as we know, very personal. It cannot help but change us and alter our direction in life. But what of the effect of a nation's bereavement? How can that affect individuals and the population as a whole? We have already seen how people reacted, and continue to react, to the deaths of Eva Peron and Vladimir Lenin, but, to me, one of the saddest examples of a nation mourning and in shock occurred with the death of Princess Diana. Diana's death is by now well documented. She, along with her boyfriend, Dodi Al-Fayed, and a driver, Henri Paul, were killed in Paris in tragic circumstances when the car they were travelling in crashed in a tunnel next to the River Seine. The only survivor was Diana's bodyguard, Trevor Rees-Jones. Diana clung to life and was only pronounced dead at the Pitie-Salpetriere Hospital at 4 a.m. on 31st August 1997. Alcohol, speed and pursuit by the press were given as possible causes of the crash, but the absolute truth may never be known.

Within minutes of Diana's death, arrangements were underway, and the Royal Family's funeral directors, the old and respected London firm Leverton's, were alerted to activate plans for her return. Some six or seven years prior to Diana's death, Kenyon's, funeral directors to the Royal Family for many years, lost that privilege when they were sold to the French funeral firm Pompes Funèbres Generales. Wanting to keep the contract local and with an old established family firm, the Royal Family then approached Leverton's. In a strange twist, however, the French company, one of the biggest in the world, were, I believe, owned by the holding company Suez Lyonnaise des Eaux, a firm encompassing water and refuse companies, in which I have been advised that the Queen holds, or held, shares. But, whatever the complicated machinations, the Leverton family are fine people and very respectable professionals.

Ironically, the French Company Pompes Funèbres Generales had, at the time of Diana's death, been acquired by Service Corporation International, a huge American Company that was now also the owners of Kenyon's, and they were the funeral directors who assisted in Diana's repatriation to England. Clive Leverton flew out to escort Diana back to Northolt Royal Airforce base. A famous photograph taken by Arthur Edwards, of the *Sun* newspaper, shows Clive Leverton walking in front of Diana's coffin, which is carried by uniformed staff of Pompes Funèbres Generales, draped in the royal colours and led by a minister of religion. Strange how these things happen. The shipping arm of Kenyon's – then Kenyon Air Transportation and now Kenyon Christopher Henley – is in part owned by Albin's so is now back in British hands. And it appears that the Queen once owned shares in the holding company that owned Pompes Funèbres Generales, the French monopoly funeral directors. As they say, the only thing stranger than life is death.

Diana's funeral has been reported in great detail, but some interesting points are not so well known. The Palace gave no official confirmation of whether or not the body had been embalmed, or whether Diana was prepared in France or England. That will have to remain confidential, but at no time was a state visitation and viewing of the body considered. During the period leading up to Diana's funeral, Leverton's gave justice to nearly 30 other funerals, all with equal respect, just as we saw with the funeral home that conducted Elvis Presley's funeral. Even for a family with over 200 years' experience, this funeral was a daunting task, and I expect they had a few sleepless nights before the event.

The flowers brought by the public to Kensington Palace lay some five feet deep, such was the nation's tribute. The bottom layer was so hot, at around 180°F, that it was turning to compost. It was the lack of space in Westminster Abbey, and not alienation from the Royal Family, that prevented Diana's burial there. It was first decided that she should be interred in the Spencer family crypt, although this was later changed to the island grave at Althorp House in Northamptonshire. The journey covered 77 miles and was led by a motorcade of half a dozen motorcycles. The hearse that carried Diana was a 1985 Daimler DS420, and when the police sergeant in charge of the motorcade saw it, he feared for its ability to make the journey. But Daimlers run forever, and several of the Queen's fleet of cars are older than that! The Daimler has, however, since been retired and is, I understand, being kept by Leverton's; after my experience with Churchill's hearse, I'm sure that is a very wise move. It is said that around 2.3 billion people viewed the funeral worldwide. Now the legend of Diana, like that of Eva Peron, continues to grow and grow.

Many of us are aware that Diana had a very big heart, which would often rule her head, probably being her biggest asset even though it sometimes caused her problems. A story has recently come to light showing Diana's caring reaction to a close friend's loss of a baby just six months into her pregnancy. Diana was so upset by this loss that she offered to help bury the baby in Kensington Palace Gardens. The grave was dug by the west wall of the garden and marked by a small vase-type urn. It is said that she gave the parents a key so that they could visit whenever they wished. A report by Alexander Hitchen in the Sunday paper *The*

People tells us that Diana referred to this part of the garden as 'my oasis'. This illustrates why the nation felt to close to her and why there was such a reaction to her death.

One of my pet hates is criticism of the funeral industry. The author Jessica Mitford, in her work and in her campaigns throughout her life, satirised the whole funeral world yet, ironically, made a great living from her book *The American Way of Death*. She had no respect for people's right to choose how they mourn, however simple or complicated. She did not like florists, floral tributes, hearses, funeral directors, caskets, memorialisation, embalming . . . If it was part of the death industry, Mitford did not like it. In her book, she advocated only simple funerals, if possible at cost price. When it was first published, quite a long time ago now, her book was ground-breaking in the US, and she was deemed a small icon by those who knew her no better. However, most Americans I have met see the book for what it was, a selfish personal view. I feel that how Diana was mourned stood for everything that Jessica Mitford did not.

At the time of Diana's death I was assisting an American company as a part-time consultant, working from time to time at their office in Jermyn Street in central London. The company employed many thousands of people nationwide, and the London base was manned mostly by Americans. The chief executive was a nice, calm man with, to an Englishman, the rather strange name of Royal Keith. It was his reaction, and that of his American staff, that truly surprised me: they were devastated. Royal wrote a letter to every member of staff and, knowing my experience with bereavement and my interest in counselling, asked me to be available for any London-based staff needing help. They visited Kensington Palace en masse with their families several times and were completely overawed by Diana's death. In a way, they considered themselves very privileged to be here at such a time. They completely closed the office for Diana's funeral even though this was a Saturday and someone was expected to be in the office to liaise with those 'stateside'. Everybody arrived early to witness Diana's final departure. I truly believe they felt they were representing not only the American public but also the American funeral industry, a chance perhaps to show its values.

At Albin's, we had a photograph of Diana and a book for people to sign that was later sent to the Royal Family with Bermondsey's condolences. Hundreds of local people added their names to it. I was truly taken back to my childhood and Churchill's death, experiencing exactly the same kind of feelings. The nation was absolutely overtaken by loss. It was almost as if the population needed a good cry and Diana's death gave it that chance. But what was unique was just how personally people took her death. When we hear that someone has died, our immediate reaction, our words to their relative, is to say how sorry we are for their loss. That's nice, and of course the correct thing to do, but is it accurate? We cannot truly feel their loss, we cannot truly be sorry; we can only be kind to them. How can we feel the pain of their loss, but how can we be truly sorry if we do not feel that pain? The other side of the coin is that if we do feel that kind of pain deeply, rather than as just a remembrance of something that once happened to us too, we may be showing a lack of adjustment to a personal bereavement. For us to be there for that person, we need to know what they are feeling without having to feel exactly what they are experiencing; more than this would drain us too much to allow us to be a support. Bereavement and grief are such personal things and always different.

But Diana's death became nationally personal to so many. People sobbed in private and in public. I found myself at the airport the day Diana died. You could feel an atmosphere of confusion and loss even then. People arrived just wanting to get out of the country. I was intrigued by this kind of panic, which I had never witnessed before. One griefstricken man was completely distraught: he wanted to buy a ticket out of the country; it seemed anywhere would do. When I tried to calm him down, he said he could not bear to face the dreadful truth, he just had to be somewhere else. He loved Diana so much that to watch the television news or read the papers was too much. I watch the signs of bereavement displayed daily as people let all their barriers down, opening up the deep-rooted grief that loss brings, but this was something new to me.

Not wanting to face death is to expected. When we are young, we close our eyes when we are afraid, hoping that if we cannot see what we are afraid of, it will go away – but it never does! Diana's death forced people to open their eyes to death and their own vulnerability in the face of death's inevitability. The mood of the country was one of overwhelming sadness; a kind of gloomy depression hung over everybody. Kensington Gardens, Diana's London home, was flooded with glorious flowers left by the people as a public display of grief and respect. In death, the lives people have lived are often seen through rose-tinted spectacles. The good things are clearer, the bad dimmer; that's just the way we are made. When we look back, the old days always seem like the good old days, yet our time will be the good old days for those who follow. And so it is with death.

Elaine, Jackie and Maureen from Albin's took some flowers themselves and went late one evening to Kensington Palace. They were stunned, not only by the flowers, but also by the silence. Thousands of people, 11 p.m., yet complete silence, a very moving experience. I think what they were witnessing was the first stage of bereavement, numbness. They had seen it every day in their work arranging funerals but had not recognised it in such mass. More than that, they too were suffering the same numbness. So who counsels the counsellors? The barrier that protects them daily was down so, for a while, they were open to the serious pain that grief brings, and that is very dangerous in their profession. Having, and showing, feelings is very important to funeral directors if they are good, but we have to carry a built-in protection.

The Thursday evening news announced that Diana would be removed from her resting place to her home in Kensington Palace. That evening, we strangely had what we called a 'church take', then heading for the airport to repatriate the deceased lady to Ireland after a Catholic Mass. I say 'strangely' because to have such a job in Kensington is unusual as we are mainly based in south London. The Irish community in Kensington is small and I had never been to this church before. As we drove slowly along Kensington High Street, adjacent to the Palace, heads turned and the word spread – 'This must be Diana coming home.' People rushed to the kerbside. It was about 7.45 p.m., and we were due in church at 8.00. Despite the very moving and exciting atmosphere, we, as always, kept our composure as I walked the final quarter of a mile to the church.

When we left the church and turned again into the High Street, the clock in the hearse showed 9.30 p.m., and early darkness was falling on the well-lit High Street. Our hearse had beautiful interior lighting, and the coffin, as with the one Diana was buried in, was made of solid oak: it looked very regal and elegant in the illumination inside the hearse. Yet again people rushed to the kerbs. The silence enfolding the grounds of Kensington Palace was broken as the word spread of 'Diana's return'. A number of photographers were desperately trying to get some photographs just in case this was Diana so I had to reassure them that it was not, even though this was every bit as important a final departure. Respecting this, we were able to proceed without further interruption.

I often think about that lady whom we returned to Ireland. She was only in her 40s and had also left two children who adored her every bit as much as Diana's sons did her. And isn't this what we should really be mourning – not that Diana was a princess, once Her Royal Highness, once the wife of the possible future King of England, not her beauty or her style, but that she was a loving mother of two fine boys who were lost to her and she to them? The lady we returned to her family in Ireland was buried on the same day as Diana, just outside Dublin in a small Catholic cemetery. Like Diana, she was surrounded by her family and true friends, probably more sure of who her true friends were than someone so much in the public eye. This lady was not famous, not able in life to reach out and touch a nation as Diana did, but she was mourned for the right reasons. Death became the great equaliser that life certainly is not.

In the months that followed Diana's death, matching the popularity of singer Elton John's version of *Candle in the Wind* was the popularity of arranging pre-paid funerals. Pre-arrangements quadrupled, and enquiries were endless. Diana's death opened people's minds to the reality of how fragile life can be and how close death always is. If death could come to someone so young, so full of life, so gorgeous, it could come to anyone.

We were reminded of this when the world again went into mourning, this time on 11th September 2001 – 9/11 – the day that changed America for ever. The terrifying events of this day must by now have been broadcast and documented in every far corner of the globe. Here, I want to look at the effect that it left on the American people and on those of us around the world who looked on in disbelief as four American passenger jets were hijacked. Two were seen on film footage as they were flown like angels of death into the World Trade Center Twin Towers in the business centre of Manhattan, New York. They immediately exploded, killing all on board and causing the towers to collapse, with thousands more innocent deaths. At the same time, two other jets were also on suicide missions, one headed for the Pentagon, the other presumed to be heading for the centre of American government, the White House, in Washington DC. All on board were again bravely lost, but the damage was minimal in comparison to the devastation endured at the centre of the Twin Towers.

In New York, it was early morning, but in the UK it was mid-afternoon and I was in my office at Culling Road. My Dad phoned from his home, where he had been watching television when the earth-shattering news broke. Within minutes, thanks to disaster camera teams and high technology, the scene of the terrorist action had been beamed to the world. I switched on my own television and watched in disbelief. I phoned my colleague Carole in Houston, who, like me, was watching the events as they unfolded. She was in tears and very difficult to console. Already I was beginning to feel a difference from other losses felt nationally and internationally. Instead of numbness, the usual first stage of bereavement, anger was immediate in everyone.

Carole is part of an emergency team working for the big American funeral conglomerate Service Corporation International. Pulling herself together and heading for work, she began to coordinate resources. Although it may seem harsh at such an emotional time, equipment and staff resources have to be made available – portable mortuaries, refrigeration allocation at local mortuaries and hospitals, body bags, emergency caskets, hygienic and sterile clothing, identification teams, dentists, pathologists, embalmers, funeral directors. All these have to be ready behind the scenes, like a fourth emergency service. While all this is being prepared, the first emergency teams are desperately trying to save lives and recover the injured and dead, others attempting to make the site safe. Ground Zero, as we would come to know it, was one of the most devastated disaster scenes I have ever seen.

You cannot truly explain to people what it is like to be at the scene of a disaster. There is a kind of organised chaos as each of the teams begins to undertake its responsibilities. As the days wear on, silence becomes the order as survivors are searched for. People like me are not usually called in for a number of days. The first thing you notice on arrival is the smell of death, a horrible smell that I can only describe, however distasteful it seems, as being like burnt lard. When I visited Ground Zero in November, some two months into the clean-up, I could still smell the odour of death hanging in the air. It was a strange, eerie place where, among the noise of bulldozers, there was a weird kind of silence. From that silence came a kind of peace, a feeling of 'Who could forget?'

Even with America's ability to overcome this attack on its way of life, Ground Zero was a shocking monument. As a nation, their first angry reaction was to consider what happened as an act of war and to take appropriate action to defend themselves against further attacks; they then began to seek retribution, both very understandable feelings, but what of the people themselves? New Yorkers pulled themselves together without delay and returned their lives to as normal a state as possible.

Death is not always the great divider: it often unites, and that is what I feel has happened here. Americans have put aside class and race issues and pulled together as one. They have been through joint national anger, and deprivation, realising just what has been lost to them. But anger and loss are only two of the commonly accepted and important stages of grief, depression, numbness and denial being the others. Perhaps there has been no time for these painful experiences so anger has overtaken all the other emotions. To me that seems dangerous and I will attempt to explain why I see it that way.

The usual first feeling of numbness allows us to prepare for the stages that will follow. Being numb protects us for a while from the painful reality of loss. Immediately experiencing anger, that powerful but dangerous emotion, denies people the opportunity to prepare for the dreadful feelings that anger brings with it. There *will* be a time for anger, but it has to be correctly directed. The body is a clock that ticks

103

in order – break the order and the precision is gone, and numbness at the right time gives us the space to prepare.

In terms of depression, many people say that it is a stage of grief we could all do without. It is certainly the most painful stage and the most dangerous of feelings, but, if it is correctly handled, coming out of depression is like rising from the ashes to realise that there is a tomorrow and a way forward, and with it great relief. Without this stage, we may not be facing the truth. Depression is inevitable in normal grief as we come to terms with our loss. The American nation should have been able to achieve this, but the anger might just have been too overwhelming and maybe not good in the long run.

Denial too is important. It is not surprising that we want to deny something as dreadful as death, and this gives us a chance openly to discuss our feelings about the loss. Denial usually follows on numbness and is the first feeling we have as we enter back into reality. The numbness, having protected us from unbearable pain, brings the truth as it wears off, and our first thoughts are to deny that this has ever happened. The denial is usually only psychological, in which we subconsciously and purposely forget that the loss has occurred, for example by preparing a meal for two instead of one. In the case of 9/11, a little denial would also have given the nation a temporary time-out and been quite healthy in the long run.

All these stages happen for a reason. Bereavement is, as I always emphasise, a very serious illness and needs careful treatment if the body and mind are to repair themselves. Feeling only the loss and the anger can be too much to bear in the long run; in the case of national grief, it is a very dangerous road to walk even for such a great country

The Albin's legacy: Fred (holding the pen), Dad and me,
with my sons Simon (top left) and Jonathan.

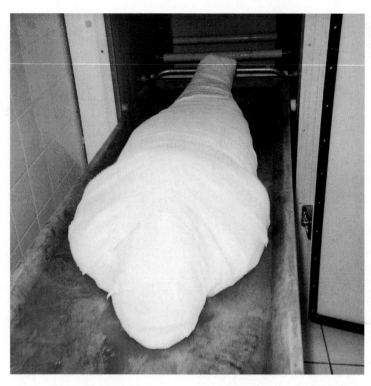

Mr Iouannou's mummified mummy.

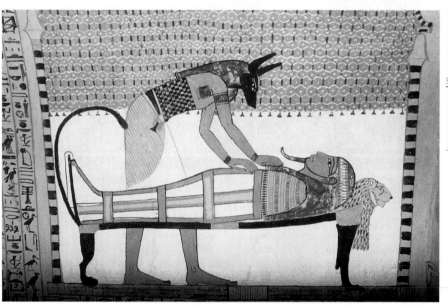

Painting from the tomb of Sennedjem at Dier el Medina, showing the
Egyptian god Anubis with the mummy of Sennedjem.

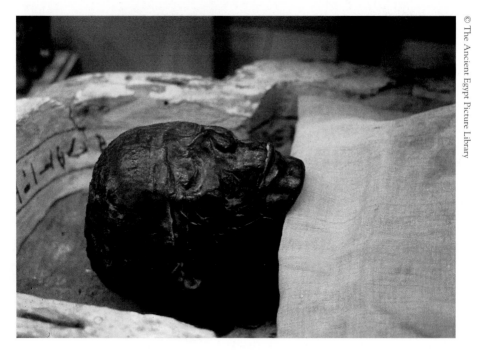

A mummy now in the collection of the Antiquities
Museum in Copenhagen.

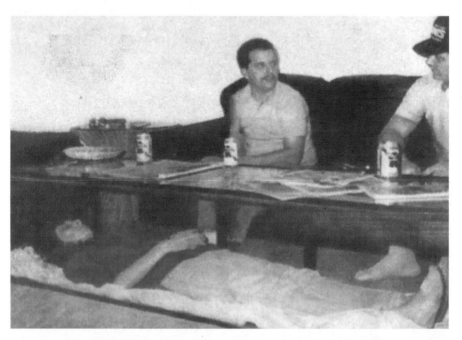

'I Love Lucy.' This woman's body was entombed in her
husband's coffee table.

A Japanese hearse with its ornate canopy.

The Motorbike Funerals Company and their motorbike hearse.

The long line of white Cadillacs forming Elvis Presley's funeral cortège.
Tearful fans line the route.

The crowds gather to watch the solemn procession of Diana, Princess of Wales' coffin through central London in September 1997.

Pete Postlethwaite as Len Green in *The Sins*.

A newly constructed cryostat.

CELESTIS

A STEP INTO THE UNIVERSE

FLIGHT CAPSULE INSCRIPTION FORM
(Please print or type)

The following name and personal message should be imprinted on the flight capsule that contains the cremated remains of _____. Contract number _____

NAME

The name will be inscribed as it appears on this form, below. Please be sure to check for the desired capitalization, spelling and punctuation.

The name is to be inscribed on the flight capsule exactly as follows:

PERSONAL MESSAGE ...be inscribed as it appears

The personal message cannot exceed 25 characters. Th... on this form. Please be sure to check for the desired c...

The message is to be inscribed on the flight capsule e...

Approved By:

Purchaser's Signature

Celestis

Celestis COMMEMORATIVE SPACEFLIGHT SERVICES

ORDER FORM

1- Purchaser Information (please print)

Title:_____ Name First:_____ Middle Initial:____ Last:_____
Address:_____ City:_____ State/Province:_____
Zip Code:_____ Country:_____ Phone (with area code):_____
Fax:_____ E-mail:_____
Name of Deceased:_____ Relation to Deceased:_____

2 - Service Selection (please check desired service)

____ Earthview Service I (price $995.00 USD) — This service launches a 1g sample of the cremated remains into earth orbit, and is deemed complete upon the attainment of one orbit around the earth.

____ Earthview Service II (price $5,300.00 USD) — This service launches a 7g sample of the cremated remains into earth orbit, and is deemed complete upon the attainment of one orbit around the earth.

____ Voyager Service (price $12,500.00 USD) — This service launches a 1g sample of the cremated remains into deep space, and is deemed complete upon the successful initiation of the propulsion out of Earth's gravitational influence.

____ Lunar Service (price $12,500.00 USD) — This service launches a 1g sample of the cremated remains to either lunar orbit or to the lunar surface, and is deemed complete upon insertion into the moon's gravitational influence.

____ Ad Astra Service (price $300.00 USD) — This service transmits a high powered digital memorial (including a photo and biography of the deceased) to the stars, and includes a certificate of Star Registry commemorating the "naming" of a star in memory of the deceased.

The *Earthview Service I, Earthview Service II, Voyager Service* and *Lunar Service* include: 1. The launch of the symbolic portion of the cremated remains into space as indicated; 2. Flight capsule imprinted with personal message (see FLIGHT CAPSULE INSCRIPTION FORM); 3. Invitations to the launch event; 4. Personalized video of the launch event and memorial ceremony; 5. Dedicated virtual memorial of the Deceased at the Celestis web site; 6. Contribution to the Celestis Foundation; 7. Performance assurance (see TERMS AND CONDITIONS below); and, 8. Sea scattering of the un-launched balance of the cremated remains with certificate (scattering is optional -- see AUTHORIZATION FOR FINAL DISPOSITION form).

3 - Payment Method (There is no sales tax charged on Celestis services)

If Paying By Check: Please make checks payable to Celestis, Inc. and mail this completed, signed form to: Celestis, Inc., ATTN: Customer Service, 2444 Times Blvd., Suite 260, Houston, Texas 77005, USA

If Paying By Credit or Debit Card: Card type (circle one) VISA AMEX MC Discover Card

Account number: _____ Expiration Date: _____
Signature: _____ Date: _____

4 - Signature

By tender of this order and payment with my signature below I hereby accept the Celestis COMMEMORATIVE SPACEFLIGHT SERVICES TERMS AND CONDITIONS.

Signature: _____ Date: _____

Page 1 of 2

To infinity and beyond? The brochure and order form of Celestis,
who can shoot your remains into space!

as America. But these are only my own, unsupported observations, and my heart and thoughts go out to the American nation as it moves forward.

Finding it in our hearts to forgive is sometimes too much to ask, but time brings changes in people, and it is only with time that we can begin to forgive and to forget, at least the pain as we should never forget those who have been lost: 'Memory is the golden chain that binds us till we meet again.' We cannot truly get over something this bad, but we have to find a way forward. If we blame generations to come for our faults, we will never find our own inner peace. The American nation may still face the stages of grief as the anger begins to wear away and it begins to repair itself after cleaning its wounds, but what I am sure that every American does feel is the great privilege of being alive. After such terrible events, life always seems far more precious. We never think something like that is going to happen to us; when 'we' become 'them', the victims, it rocks our own stupid thoughts of immortality. An American funeral director colleague sent me the following words, maybe a little oversentimental in British terms but clearly showing what was important before 11th September and what is truly important now.

Twenty-five ways we're different this Christmas:

1. Last Christmas, we were thinking about all the things we didn't have; this Christmas, we are thinking about all the things we do have.
2. Last Christmas, we were placing wreaths on the doors of our homes; this Christmas, we are placing wreaths on the graves of our heroes.

3. Last Christmas, we were letting our sons play with toy guns; this Christmas, we are teaching them that guns are not toys.

4. Last Christmas, we were counting our money; this Christmas, we are counting our blessings.

5. Last Christmas, we paid lip service to the real meaning of the holidays; this Christmas, we are paying homage to it.

6. Last Christmas, we were lighting candles to decorate; this Christmas, we are lighting candles to commemorate.

7. Last Christmas, we were digging deep into our bank accounts to find money to fly home for the holidays; this Christmas, we are digging deep into our souls to find the courage to do so.

8. Last Christmas, we were trying not to let annoying relatives get the best of us: this Christmas, we are trying to give the best of ourselves to them.

9. Last Christmas, we thought it was enough to celebrate the holidays; this Christmas, we know we must also find ways to consecrate them.

10. Last Christmas we thought a man who could rush down a football field was a hero; this Christmas, we know a man who rushes into a burning building is the real one.

11. Last Christmas, we were thinking about the madness of the holidays; this Christmas, we are thinking about the meaning of them.

12. Last Christmas, we were getting on one another's nerves; this Christmas, we are getting on our knees.

13. Last Christmas, we were giving thanks for gifts from stores; this Christmas, we are giving thanks for gifts from God.

14. Last Christmas, we were wondering how to give our children all the things that money can buy – the hottest toys, the latest fashions, the newest gadgets; this Christmas, we are wondering how to give them all the things it can't – a sense of security, safety, peace.

15. Last Christmas, we were thinking about all the pressure we are under at the office; this Christmas, we are thinking about the people who no longer have an office to go to.

16. Last Christmas, we were singing carols; this Christmas, we are singing anthems.

17. Last Christmas, we were thinking how good it would feel to be affluent; this Christmas, we are thinking how good it feels to be alive.

18. Last Christmas, we thought angels were in heaven; this Christmas, we know some are right here on earth.

19. Last Christmas, we were contemplating all the changes that we wanted to make in the New Year; this Christmas, we are contemplating all the changes we will have to make in this new reality.

20. Last Christmas, we believed in the power of the pocketbook; this Christmas, we believe in the power of prayer.

21. Last Christmas, we were sharing/spreading/listening to the gossip; this Christmas, we are sharing/spreading/listening to the gospel.

22. Last Christmas, we were complaining about how much of our earnings went to pay taxes; this Christmas, we comprehend that freedom isn't free.

23. Last Christmas, we valued things that were costly; this Christmas, we value things that are holy.

24. Last Christmas, the people we idolised wore football,

basketball and baseball uniforms; this Christmas, the people we idolise wear police, firefighter and military uniforms.

25. Last Christmas, 'Peace on earth' is something we prayed for on Sunday mornings; now it is something we pray for every day.

There is one thing we must always keep in mind, 'FREEDOM IS NOT FREE'
Merry Christmas! May the beauty of the season bring joy to your heart!

Freedom is an essential part of the American constitution, and American citizens will correctly defend it to the end, but what happened brought great fear, not only to America, but to the whole world. For at least a year, people were afraid to fly, with huge economic consequences for the airline, travel and insurance industries and a knock-on effect on many, many businesses, including our repatriation work. Now, the situation is beginning to repair itself as people again find the courage to travel and slowly begin to invest with some confidence.

At the beginning of November 2002, we were called to the airport to receive the remains of another person found in the debris of Ground Zero. After taking the deceased to the coroner (a legal requirement by law when a deceased person is repatriated to the UK) for yet another inquest, we drove the deceased, in a casket in a private ambulance, to his family in Middlesbrough so that they could say goodbye together as a family. That family, still thoughtful of others, considered themselves one of the lucky ones who got the chance to have a personal funeral. Some will never have that chance because those they loved and lost that day will never be found. Seeing is believing, and believing helps you to move on, and I have a feeling that we could be receiving remains well into the future, such is the dedication of those still working at the scene. For the dead who will never be found, Ground Zero will be a memorial to their memory for eternity, whatever is finally built there. Time passes but true love remains.

7

The grand tour

We often say things without thinking. I was recently at the Eltham Crematorium in south London conducting a local funeral. At the end of the service, I went into the music room to collect the family's CD, which had been played during the service. There, waiting for the next service, was Dennis, a local humanist and a very gentle, thoughtful person. 'Hi Barry', he called, 'I'm with you tomorrow on the Jones funeral; are you conducting that one?' 'God willing', I replied. Now, what was I thinking saying that to a humanist? 'Not necessarily, Barry!', Dennis responded, and we smiled, understanding each other's point of view. Tolerance is everything in life – and especially in death. On my travels around the world, and having navigated the incredibly interesting maze of international funeral practices, some so very different from our own, I have learned to respect and accept the range of funeral cultures, but not without question or investigation. Some are very strange, others very funny and even a little macabre.

FINAL DEPARTURES

In the early 1990s, I became involved in a television programme called *Off the Back of a Lorry*. I have to admit to being a little naïve in thinking only the best of the media. I assisted them with some contacts I had in Italy, gave an interview and supplied a simple cremation coffin, the bottom of our range. The idea was that they would travel around Europe with different English products comparing the quality and selling possibilities. Anyway, off they went for some six weeks travelling around Europe. My basic coffin was for the Italian section. Having completed the programme, they returned to give me back the coffin and carry out a short interview to hear what I thought of Italian coffins. I was very complimentary; after all, I had always loved Italy and their home-grown goods – Sophia Loren, Gina Lollobrigida . . .

But two months later, the 30-minute section covering my coffin and the funeral manufacturing plant in Italy was shown. I sat with my mouth open as Mr Ferrari compared my basic bottom-of-the-range coffin with his highly polished, solid oak, hand-carved Italian version. He said ours was 'bloody rubbish' – not real wood, not highly polished, not as strong or as solid as his. What he failed to mention though was that the Italian oak coffin was seven times more expensive. I was more than a little cross: had I known it was a competition, I would have sent my best Royal-type coffin. But it was not long before I saw the funny side. When I met Mr Ferrari some years later, I told him what I thought of his comments. Although he had not seen the programme, he clearly remembered his remarks, and after three bottles of wine and many happy hours of eating, we were in hysterics and have since become good friends.

The Italians manufacture very beautiful coffins, many of which I now have in my own range. Indeed, we import about a thousand of them every year for ourselves and other funeral directors. The Italians also, however, have some strange customs that are practised, to what extent I do not know, on the island of Sicily. What I will describe next I have witnessed on film as well as heard when interviewing an Italian friend for an article I wrote in an international funeral magazine.

When a death occurs in Sicily, the family will undertake the usual funeral rites – a Catholic Mass, the viewing of the deceased and the choosing of a beautiful Italian coffin. This is transported to a cemetery situated on a hill. The deceased is then placed into a vault and left for a number of years, the vault being only rented due to the lack of space on the island for burial. On a given date, the coffin is removed from the vault, and the deceased is removed from the coffin by a man dressed in a short-sleeved shirt, trousers, a green apron – and pink washing-up type gloves. The family gather round as the body is removed, with some degree of ceremony, from the coffin by this man. The body is then, in front of the family, cleaned with a brush and placed upright in the ground under a slab to dry. After a few months, the family returns. The 'Marigold man' (as I like to call him) removes the slab and lifts the body to see whether it has dried enough; if not, it is replaced and the procedure is repeated a month later. When the body is sufficiently dry, it is removed and placed on a stone slab for the family to inspect. I know I could not bear to view someone I loved in that condition, but we are all different and this seems to be an old, accepted method of final departure in Sicily, people regarding it as a great honour to be present.

After the final inspection, the deceased is prepared for storage by first placing each bone, cleaning off the loose skin and dusting it with a brush. The Marigold man then holds up the bones for all to inspect the cleanness of his work. Having satisfied the family that all is present and correct, he places the bones in a clean white sheet that is then folded neatly. The sheet, with the bones enclosed within it, is placed on a private shelf, and there it stays. One year later, the family returns. The Marigold man, still dressed for the occasion, lifts down the sheet and bones, unwraps them and again cleans them with a brush. The bones are then wrapped in a new sheet and placed back on the shelf until the next anniversary.

People seem very comfortable with this repeating ceremony. The shelf is rented, and if the rent is, for whatever reason, not paid, the bones are removed, I am told, to a communal bonery underground. This way, people have the right to burial from generation to generation, one dead person making way for the next. A never-ending final departure, and one that we all need to respect and learn from.

A similar problem of space affects Madrid, where, on a hill above the M30, a 10-lane motorway, lies the Tanatorio, the city's communal morgue, where all go to await clearance. It is run by a company set up in the 1990s by the mayor of that time and now operates a virtual monopoly in Madrid. This is not a place of great elegance or tranquillity; quite the contrary – it is more like a terminus. The Tanatorio is the place where friends and family gather to pay their last respects and have a peep at the deceased before they leave.

As you arrive, you are greeted by television screens that instruct you to the correct viewing lounge. 'Body 2018 Martinez now viewing in lounge 52', the screen may declare. There is a cash machine, bar, restaurant and vending machines for phone cards and the like. Funeral trade magazines are scattered around for all to read. People just turn up, and before you know it you have a kind of party atmosphere. The elderly, perhaps not wishing to pay restaurant prices, bring bags of food and drink for their guests to enjoy. The great lack of space in the city has been overcome by the building of high-rise cemetery blocks. Each niche stands six tiers high and is leased to a particular family for 99 years. These have become so popular that it is now rare to find a soil burial. But what happens after this time has elapsed? Perhaps the family could extend the lease for another 99 years, or will they suffer the same end as the Sicilians and go to a bonery? Unfortunately, I will not be around to find out.

Like the Sicilians, the Greeks view it as acceptable to regularly exhume bodies even though it is neither legal nor possible to cremate them. Also, like the Sicilians, Athenians follow what seems to be a traumatic procedure for removing the bones from the ground. At the Zografou Cemetery, graves are leased for three years, after which a bone removal certificate is issued and the family may attend when the grave-digger crudely removes the bones and puts them into bone boxes. These are placed on the edge of the pathways like little houses. Many have lanterns and at night offer a street-like impression to those passing by.

This Greek bone-remover also has special gloves for the task, although he seems to complete his work in a more nonchalant manner, cigarette in mouth and mobile phone at the graveside. Starting with a pickaxe, he breaks the stone and border of the grave and then, digging down, removes the bones one by one into a waiting wheelbarrow. Some of the bones are still enshrouded by bits of burial gown, which he then removes like stripping a plaster from a wound. There is, of course, still the odd piece of flesh too, which is discarded, along with the burial gown, on to a rubbish pile. After about an hour, the bone-remover declares his job done and tells the family to return in 20 days for the placing of the bones in their new home on a pathway.

Not all Greeks want this of course, but there is no choice, as the Greek Orthodox Church has declared this will be so whatever one's religion or choice of final departure. This has to be accepted or the body removed from the country. There is a large movement for change and for the acceptance of cremation, but this has not yet been successful even though the current practice seems to be contrary to people's human rights. Despite widespread lobbying by many international and Greek advocators of cremation, the government just seems to close its eyes to the problem. To add insult to injury, a special charge is levied on the family for this procedure, and a large tip is expected by the bone-removal man. Surely, people should at the very least be able to have this basic human right of choice, the freedom to decide how they are finally laid to rest?

Some individuals seem to choose the most unlikely methods of departure. In the hills of Tennessee, in the good old US of A, there stands a farm like no other you will ever find, for this is the 'Dead Farm'. The requirements for a job here ought to be a lack of sense of smell, a strong stomach, not being squeamish, a head for figures (because

116

no one here has a name), and the lack of a sense of humour because the job is not at all funny. The Dead Farm receives bodies donated from all over America for research purposes, but the research carried out here is not your everyday medical research. Instead, the farm is a kind of centre for forensic science, a black hill for the study of decay. When a body is donated, it is brought freshly to the farm often only hours after legal death. The bodies are catalogued and numbered: the record might read 'Corpse 1084: black male, aged 50 years, died 17th November 2002 at New York Medical Centre, cause of death: heart attack, weight 200 kilos, preservation: none undertaken, medical records in life: attached, name of deceased: Robert Jones (or withheld).' Mr Jones, henceforth corpse 1084, is now officially a resident of the farm.

In a medical school, a corpse would be preserved and kept for students to learn their anatomy on first hand. On the farm, however, the corpses are laid, some clothed, some unclothed, in different positions (face down, crawling, lying on their backs). Some will be completely in the open, others under shallow earth. They are inspected daily for temperature change and logged for signs and timing of deterioration. In short, they are left to putrefy. The gases build up until the body bursts and then begins to dry out, some of them almost mummifying as they dehydrate. At this point, the successful applicant for a job here has to pick the remaining skin from the corpse, dismantle the skeleton and place the bones in a cleaning machine that will blow off any remaining tissue. The bones are then weighed, measured, calcium-tested and again logged.

But what happens to these data? All the information is entered into a computer program that will, when completed, hold pathology information and secrets from thousands of corpses on the farm. This will assist criminal investigation worldwide. How? Let's say that a corpse, a possible murder victim, is found in shallow ground. By entering the type of ground in which the corpse was found, the height, weight, sex, age, race, time of year, average heat and so on, the program will be able to determine the date and time of death, possibly even to the hour. That kind of information, if accurate, can be invaluable to a murder enquiry. But what of the final departure of our make-believe corpse 1084? Well, his bones would be placed in a box, labelled and stored in a modern bonery, a warehouse with thousands of others, in case they could be, as police investigators might say, of further assistance in enquiries.

Others have different ideas of how they would like to be treated when they die. The Australians, often labelled chauvinistic, are the first nation to have a funeral service run solely by women. This advertises itself as 'White Lady Funeral Service'. Within five years of opening its first funeral home (called a chapel in Australia), in Adelaide in 1987, they had established chapels in Sydney, Brisbane, Melbourne and Canberra, a massive growth even by their parent company's standards. Today, some 15 years on, they have a princely 24 outlets across Australia.

The 'white ladies' are exactly that; the service is run by women wearing white suits, with reddish-brown hats and matching gloves and shoes. Everything is white – the caskets, the hearse, the limousines, the flowers. Certainly one up on a white Christmas or a white wedding. But the company has been an amazing success in Australia, describing how 'White Lady Funerals grew out of a simple realisation that the calm strength of women could offer a special kind of support to grieving families' and that 'White Lady offers a refreshing and unique approach to the funeral service'.

How would we, in the UK, regard such a service – would we see it as sexist, as prejudiced against men? That would certainly put the boot on the other foot. At Albin's we have some wonderful women – and, let's be honest, they are the world's true, natural carers – but I could not imagine Albin's without men as well. The mix of approaches seems to me the best to offer.

So having looked at a few of the options on offer, let's take a whistle-stop tour round the world to take a peek at some of the odder situations that have arisen in other countries. Returning to Spain, we might want to visit Christopher Columbus, buried in Seville Cathedral. Nothing strange about that, but he had previously also received no fewer than four final send-offs in Spain and Cuba. It seems that he was, even in death, a great traveller. The story does not end there either: there is so much controversy about where he is truly buried that the authorities are about to open all five burial spots to find the truth.

Further across Europe, Sir Anthony Hopkins truly upset the residents of Prague, Czechoslovakia, when filming his movie *Black Sheep*, affecting the day-to-day life of Prague's biggest cemetery and delaying some funerals while filming was taking place. Sir Anthony had also been parking his trailer in the crematorium, spooking the locals, who had not forgotten his amazing role as Hannibal Lecter in the film *Silence of the Lambs*. High-speed chases around the cemetery, a place that usually reflects peace and tranquillity, upset local families too. Although the film is said to be a comedy, I'm sure no one was laughing in Prague.

Our next stop is New Zealand and a man who has been labelled a serial mourner, rather than, like Anthony Hopkins' character, a serial killer. This man, it is reported, has been to over 200 funerals in the past 20 years, and has now been banned by his own family from any further appearances (with the exception of his own, of course). It seems that he scans the newspapers for information about forthcoming funerals and then just turns up. Maybe it is time for him to join the profession instead.

Another man thoroughly enjoying his role at the end of life is a Californian sculptor who specialises in urns for the storage of ashes – but with a difference. These urns have strobe lights, moving parts and music to match: it could only happen in Hollywood. In this extrovert world of Tinseltown, immortality is often striven for but rarely, if ever, found. The late, great Humphrey Bogart was buried with a whistle inscribed with his wife Lauren Bacall's legendary line 'If you need anything, just whistle.' Truly romantic, but I hope I never hear it.

Staying in the States, the American writer Truman Capote took his philosophy to the very limits after his own final departure. He was cremated, not an unusual occur-rence in itself, but Truman spoke from the grave through his Will. He left his cremated remains, his ashes, to be divided in equal shares, one half to his life companion and the other half to the talk show host Johnny Carson. Johnny kept his at home on the mantelpiece until 1998 when they were stolen from a party he was hosting and never returned. I am sure he would love them back if they are ever found.

It is not just people who are cherished to this degree. A pet memorial park in Los Angeles offers full funerals, hearse, casket, grave, grave memorial stones and mausoleums. Most interestingly, there is also a bereavement counselling service for those who have lost pets, be they fish or elephants. Loss is painful, and those who have lost a pet can suffer genuine feelings of grief, albeit to a more extreme degree than we would expect to find in our own country.

Such loss is approached in a slightly different way in South America, acknowledging the sacred nature of both body and soul. As I mentioned in an earlier chapter, the Mexican people celebrate the Day of the Dead in a lovely time of remembrance on 1st and 2nd November each year. Families bake special bread and take food, drink, flowers and candles to the cemetery to commemorate the souls of all those family members who have departed. It is believed that the souls of adults and children alike return to their homes, a wonderful feeling for those who truly believe in this connection with the dead.

San Bernardo, near Bogotá in Colombia, is also the scene of some amazing events. People who die in this mystical place are never embalmed as it does not seem to be necessary: the dead apparently mummify naturally in their coffins. It has become so popular that people visit from all over to see this spectacle for themselves; the Colombians have even opened a museum where the best bodies are kept, not that I would want my final resting place to be a museum. Despite making enquiries, I have not yet been able to find out what causes this mummification – is it something in the local climate, a miracle, dehydration? The answer will have to wait, but I have added Colombia to my own list of places to visit so that I can find out what happens.

And so we return to the UK, to Scotland first, where an inventive fellow, by trade a cabinet-maker, has designed a range of bookcases and wardrobes that convert, when you need them, into coffins. I am not sure though what happens to your books or clothes at this point.

In Ireland, also making the most of resources, one particular funeral director is now offering coffins and caskets for rental, but only it seems for cremation. He lines the interior of the coffin or casket with a cardboard box, like a cocoon, which is removed, with the deceased in it, at the point of cremation, the rented outer portion of the coffin being returned to be rented again. This option has also been available from us in London for 15 years or more, but no one has truly ever required it.

One wet Monday morning in October 2002, another Irish encounter gave me something to think about, reminding me yet again that you can never stand on your laurels in this profession, that you never know what will happen when the phone rings. At the other end of the telephone, a very fast Irish accent said, 'I want you to come and get my brother and take him to your Dead House.'

In Ireland, 'the Dead House' is a not uncommon expression for the funeral home, a charming, honest and accurate description of a place where the dead are kept. It is surely a more explicit term than others we use: the undertakers, the funeral home, the funeral shop, the funeral supermarket. For our culture, however, the term is a bit direct. We all feel that we have to take the edge off the truth: 'passed away', 'departed this life', 'fell asleep'. These are ways in which we, in our society, describe the death of a person. Would it not be best to simply say, 'He died'; after all, that's the truth, isn't it? Are we trying to hide the truth or simply break it gently? What is good for some people is bad for others so we just have to judge each situation as it comes. Even for someone like me, with so much experience of the field, there never seems to be an absolute right or wrong. But that is what makes a good funeral director – an ability to feel naturally the needs of a family in grief, and not just a diploma to say someone knows the right procedures. In my usual football terms, it is a case of if you don't have the gift, the tactics won't help. But I still cannot imagine putting an advertisement in the *Yellow Pages* saying 'Albin's Dead House, Open all hours (don't forget to call).'

What followed this telephone call was a three-day invasion of our 'Dead House' by a family of travellers, polite, in control, organised, easy to deal with and above all honourable, paying every penny of their debt. They appointed one person who controlled the family. He was in charge throughout, no one (and I mean no one) questioning him. A funeral such as this sort of runs itself; you just have to be there when you are wanted and stand back when they want you to. They always have a beautiful coffin, a hearse and three or four limousines. In this case, they spent the whole day with the body, hundreds of people coming and going from the Dead House every hour. They played his favourite music, spoke to him and left his favourite things – cigarettes, a can of Guinness and photos of his family. It was lovely. At 4.30 in the afternoon, we all left in procession to the Church, where the family carried the coffin in for a reception and for the body to rest overnight.

The next morning we collected the coffin and proceeded to meet the family at the home so they could again follow to the church for a Mass. After a long service with maybe 600 people coming and going, we left for the local cemetery. Over 50 vehicles followed, most of them vans, and about half a mile from the cemetery we all stopped and walked behind the hearse for the final distance. Some of the children walked alongside me. One asked me if the glass crystal on my stick was a diamond and could he hold it for a moment. This I let him do; he was thrilled and began to imitate me, not in jest but in respect for my duty. He quickly returned the stick and told me I was *cool*, very flattering for a 52-year-old! At the cemetery, they carried the coffin to the graveside, blessed it and lowered it down. The prayers now over, the grave was filled in by the men, a wooden cross placed at the head and the flowers placed on top. The priest and ourselves were given a big thank you before we adjourned to the pub for a long night. For the Irish, dealing with grief largely means joining in the funeral rites throughout, a very healthy approach! They say that the only difference between an Irish wake and an Irish wedding is one less drink.

So we are now back in London, in our own culture and traditions, but sometimes our own views are challenged in unexpected and unpleasant ways in people's choice of what they want to happen to them once they have died. Throughout this book, I have tried to raise the question of where we should draw the line of correctness when dealing with death. If one thing is acceptable, what about another? Do we all draw the line in a slightly different place? Although it seems tasteless, is the Dead Farm research facility appropriate because of the scientific information it is uncovering? Are the burial traditions in Sicily appropriate as we need to respect other cultures? Whatever we might think about these, for me, the situation I am going to describe strayed well beyond what is at all acceptable.

On Wednesday 20th November 2002, London witnessed what I consider to be an open display of unnecessary, and distasteful, butchery – the public autopsy of a 72-year-old man – the like of which has not been seen for 170 years. If death is the last great taboo and respect its guardian, as I believe it is, Gunther Von Hagen's public autopsy of this poor man was indeed a showman's attempt to destroy it. We live in a world where people demand to know the truth in detail, and in my writing I have always tried to give that but, I hope, never without respect and sensitivity. Von Hagen, a German living in London, is also responsible for much of the work in the Bodyworlds exhibition I mentioned in an earlier chapter. Out of 2000 people who tried to get tickets, the 500 who attended were charged £12 each to view the post mortem. Television companies paid for the viewing rights, one and half million viewers watching on television.

The Murder Act of the mid-1700s ordered that executed murderers be dissected, reinforcing the severity of their crime and offering a final cruel humiliation to their final departure. In those dark distant years, high treason too was punished by dissection or dismemberment and, the highest indignity, the exhibition of the body parts on gates and walls for all to see, a grim end. But what had this poor unfortunate man done to deserve his humiliation? He had died some eight months previously and had been preserved in formalin so the autopsy was in fact completely unrealistic. The normal task of a post mortem technician, a skilful and very respectful breed, is at best very unpleasant. Had the post mortem been true to death, with a fresh corpse and modern tooling, the 500 keen voyeurs would have been feeling very sick, I promise you. There are natural smells created in life that are in death anything but natural, and gassy odours that can cause you to vomit. But all that emanated from this old gentleman was a gentle whiff of formalin.

And what of our elderly gentleman's final departure? He's off to Germany to be plasticised for the future. However much I disprove of the autopsy, I know that, in both life and in death, a little humour often saves the day so I was amused to read in a Sunday newspaper that Professor Von Hagen loves his wife 'to bits' – not good news for her, then!

So now we have finished our world travels. I do not know whether travelling on the same aircraft as me would make you feel comfortable or decidedly nervous. You might feel that death follows me around, although I have never felt this myself. On the other hand, if you can see me, you have nothing to worry about – you're still in this world!

In the late 1990s, I returned from a business trip in Argentina. It was a 14-hour flight and on arrival at Heathrow I was informed that we would not be allowed to leave the plane for some time. Little did I know the reason – a man had died midway through the journey. You often hear the call 'Is there a doctor in the house?' but never 'Is there an undertaker?' so I did not know at the time what was going on.

If someone dies in mid-flight, the pilot has a responsibility to ascertain the possible cause of death or at least have a doctor examine the deceased before anybody leaves the plane. All those on board must give their details to the airline, for example where they are travelling to and finally staying. You are also obliged to report any sickness felt within the following 48 hours without delay. In our case, collecting the information took around two hours, and in that time we were not allowed any further food or drink. There are of course very good reasons for these precautions – a virus could be spread if people were not checked, the cause could be a form of food poisoning that might need to be isolated, or death could be the result of foul play. In this case, the unfortunate gentleman had suffered a heart attack. We never know when death will strike, but, as Benjamin Franklin put it, 'There are only two certainties in life, death and taxes.' For this man, when he boarded the flight from Buenos Aires to London, he did not know it truly would be his final departure in this life.

8
The path to sainthood

My Nan would often say that anyone needed the patience of a saint to look after me, a bit harsh I thought, but then I didn't have to look after the eight-year-old me! People often use these old sayings without thinking. It is easy to see where the phrase 'patience of a saint' came from – the goodness and understanding associated with the saints, where else? But were the saints all patient and understanding, or were their lives, like ours, difficult, confusing and frustrating, full of questions without answers? Did all their patience, as I believe, truly come from faith, and doesn't faith hold the balance between this world and the next? This is confusing, I know, but it is important to our understanding of what makes a saint in life and death, how saints are made and the mystique surrounding the investigations of their remains for sainthood. I write this not as a theological expert but as an individual – and a funeral director – expressing his experience and feelings. As both an undertaker and a Catholic, I have become very aware of how important the saints' human remains are to their being accorded sainthood and hence to my own, and others' faith.

I want to concentrate here on one saint, Saint Bernadette, and the vision of 'Our Lady of Lourdes', as a model to help us understand sainthood. Not growing up a Catholic, I had no understanding of the saints. When I first heard of Our Lady of Lourdes, I seem to remember thinking that she was the lady who looked after the Lord's cricket ground at St John's Wood (a bit like, aged seven and with a fertile imagination, I thought that Wolverhampton Wanderers football team were for some reason part of the Walls Ice Cream company).

But when I became a Roman Catholic in the late 1980s, I began to realise the effect that saints such as Bernadette had on people's lives. Then, when my friend Father Alan McLean invited me to help him on a pilgrimage to Lourdes, I was, to say the least, apprehensive, but friendship prevailed and I agreed, more to help than for my own satisfaction. We were escorting a party of about 50 local people, many of them needing assistance and the security of a friendly face and helping hand. Three of us led the group – Father Alan, John, a local doctor, and myself, the undertaker. At least all eventualities were covered, which caused many a giggle in the group and fuelled much evening entertainment. We were also quite proud to be so well endowed with strong professional leaders.

I truly did not know what to expect from this pilgrimage. The only time that I had ever been away with a group other than on a school trip was on a football tour, very different, I thought! I had not expected, and was amazed and delighted to experience, the same kind of camaraderie that you get on a football trip (but with better language, of course). People unite and become one on pilgrimages. In a unique way, the group leaders become the group parents, everyone expecting to be protected, organised and spiritually led. It is wonderful as you all take responsibility for each other and begin to pull together. By the end of the week, if you have enjoyed good, all-round leadership, you begin to feel bonded and special. Over and above this, however, you have the magic of Lourdes, which has its own small daily miracles to be experienced by all. My life was more enriched than I ever thought possible from my visit to Lourdes.

When you arrive in Lourdes, a small but busy town at the foot of the Pyrenees mountains in south-west France, it all seems a little disconcerting and commercial. There are three parts to Lourdes: the old town, which contains shops, houses and the ubiquitous McDonalds fast-food emporium; the new town, with its souvenir shops and hotels; and the piece of the Domain run by the Church. Within Lourdes, there is also an area called the City of the Poor, where impoverished pilgrims can stay very cheaply and spend time in prayer on a very low budget. The town itself has about 16,000 residents, some five million pilgrims arriving each year by road, rail and air, along with 100,000 volunteers, including doctors, nurses and assistants. Around 400,000 people pass through the baths annually. As you enter the water, there is a special prayer to read: Jesus, Joseph and Mary pray for me (but before you get to 'Joseph' the temperature of the water takes your breath away, believe me!). Each day, 52 Masses are celebrated, in a variety of languages, and an average of 800 tons of candles are burned every season.

My first thoughts on seeing the town were, get me out of here! There were endless hotels and cafés, and shop upon shop selling very similar gifts – statues of Our Lady, holy water bottles, candles, clocks, rosaries, priests' vestments, tacky souvenirs, altogether a little over the top. But as you walk down through the town, towards the gates of St Joseph that lead to the beautiful upper and lower basilica overlooking the Domain, where the candlelight processions pass every evening, and then along the River Gave to the Sanctuary of the Grotto of Masabielle, you are captivated by the natural silence that prevails.

It was not until the first evening, when I first experienced this special peace, that I was able to open my mind and begin to understand and absorb the atmosphere that shrouds the real heart of Lourdes. Father Alan was the perfect person to be with when experiencing Lourdes for the first time. On another pilgrimage to Lourdes many years earlier, he had witnessed the death of his favourite aunt, who was consequently buried there. He regards her death in Lourdes, and her burial there, as a blessing and visits her grave without fail when he is in the town.

I was so taken with the candlelight procession, the music, the faith and the unity of thousands of like-minded Catholics sharing one belief that I stood apart from the procession on the second night and phoned home so that I could share the moment. That night's emotion will never leave me, in this life or the next. I left that first pilgrimage with my faith a little stronger and many new friendships to cherish. I knew I would return again and again, which I have. Each time, my feelings are the same. Thousands of sick people are taken in wheelchairs to the grotto, hoping for a miracle, yet each one of them is, through the power that brought them there, already part of a much bigger miracle than anyone can find with faith in Lourdes. To me, the true miracle of Lourdes is not the claims of cure (not that I decry any of these) but quite simply the fact that millions of people travel all because a 14-year-old, illiterate peasant girl asked them to do so.

On one trip to Lourdes, I experienced a remarkable event, a miracle, who can say what it was? Technically speaking, before any happening can be deemed a 'miracle', there is a long enquiry, and in this matter the Church is very prudent. The term 'cure' is, however, acceptable, and by the end of 1998, nearly 7000 declarations of cures had been recorded in the archives of the medical bureau of Lourdes.

Anyway, in our group was a remarkable, autistic young teenage boy called Taylor, who loves Lourdes and is a joy to travel with. He used to be taken by his devoted grandmother and aunt, but when his grandmother sadly died in late 2002, Taylor's parents allowed him to go again to Lourdes with his aunt and the group. On our earlier pilgrimage together, I took responsibility for him as we walked the Stations of the Cross, reading for him at each Station the description of the stages. Standing Taylor between my arms with the book in my hands in front of us, I began to read slowly. At first, Taylor followed every word I read – at the time, he was not able to read clearly although he could understand many words. As I began to read the third stage, Taylor, incredibly, began to read with me, and by the sixth stage he was reading alone, fluently and without help, as if he had received a gift or something inside him had suddenly come alive. Everyone was in floods of tears. Taylor and I have never forgotten the bond we forged that day, and that bright loving boy will always have a special place in my heart. He may have been born autistic, but he has a multitude of special gifts that will guide him through life.

And what of Bernadette, the girl who, at a similar age to Taylor, received the mystical visions that brought all this about and were to affect the lives of millions? Born Bernadette Soubirous in 1844, she belonged to a family of six who moved from place to place, each worse than the previous one. Bernadette was the eldest of the four children. Because of their miserable poverty, she never ate well and became a sickly child with little or no education. But she had her prayers, her family love and her rosary to comfort her. Bernadette was to receive 18 visitations from Our Lady, Mary, the Mother of Christ, which I will list as I understand them.

Thursday 11th February 1858: the meeting

Accompanied by her sister and a friend, Bernadette went to Masabielle on the banks of the River Gave to collect stones and dead wood. Removing her socks in order to cross the stream, she heard a noise like a gust of wind, and looked up towards the grotto: 'I saw a lady dressed in white; she wore a white dress and an equally white veil, a blue belt and a yellow rose on each foot.' Bernadette made the Sign of the Cross and said a rosary with the lady, who suddenly vanished when the prayer ended.

Sunday 14th February: the holy water

In spite of the fact that Bernadette's parents had forbidden her to go to the grotto, she felt an inner force drawing her there. After much insistence, her mother allowed her to go. After the first decade of the rosary, the same lady appeared. She shook holy water at her. The lady smiled and bent her head, again disappearing when the rosary ended.

Thursday 18th February: the lady speaks

On this day, Bernadette held out a pen and paper, asking the lady to write her name, but she replied, 'It is not necessary', adding, 'I do not promise to make you happy in this world but in the other. Would you be kind enough to come here for a fortnight?'

Friday 19th February: a short and silent apparition

Bernadette cames to the grotto with a lighted, blessed candle; this is the origin of carrying candles and lighting them in front of the grotto.

Saturday 20th February: silence

The lady taught her a personal prayer and, at the end of the vision, which only Bernadette could see or hear, Bernadette was overcome with a great sadness.

Sunday 21st February: 'Aquero'

The lady appeared to Bernadette very early in the morning, in the presence of about a hundred other people. Afterwards, the Police Commissioner, Jacomet, questioned Bernadette to find out what she had seen, but Bernadette would only speak of 'Aquero' (that).

Tuesday 23rd February: the secret

Surrounded by 150 other people, Bernadette arrives at the grotto, the apparition revealing to her a secret 'only for her alone'.

Wednesday 24th February: penance

The lady's message to Bernadette was: 'Penance! Penance! Penance! Pray to God for sinners. Kiss the ground as an act of penance for sinners!'

Thursday 25th February: the spring

By now, more people were becoming curious, 300 people accompanying Bernadette, who related, 'She told me to go, drink of the spring . . . I only found a little muddy water. At the fourth attempt I was able to drink. She also made me eat the herbs that were found near the spring; then the vision left and went away.' When the crowd asked, 'Do you think she is mad doing things like that?', Bernadette responded: 'It is for sinners.'

Saturday 27th February: silence

A crowd of 800 were present on this day. The apparition was silent, Bernadette drinking the water from the spring and carrying out her usual acts of penance.

Sunday 28th February: penance

Over a thousand people were present at the ecstasy. Bernadette prayed, kissed the ground and moved on her knees as a sign of penance. She was then taken to the house of Judge Ribes, who threatened her with prison for heresy.

Monday 1st March: the first miracle

Over one and a half thousand people, for the first time including a priest, assembled. During the night, Catherine Latapie, a friend of Bernadette's from Lourdes, went to the grotto, plunged her dislocated arm into the spring water and felt her hand and arm regain their movement.

Tuesday 2nd March: message to the priests

The crowd was now becoming larger and larger. The lady said to Bernadette, 'Go tell the priests to come here in procession and to build a chapel here.' Bernadette told Father Peyramale, the parish priest of Lourdes, who demanded to know the lady's name. He also asked for a sign: to see the wild rose bush on which the lady stood during her appearances to Bernadette flowering at the grotto in the middle of winter.

Wednesday 3rd March: a smile

At 7 in the morning, in the presence of 3000, Bernadette arrived at the grotto, but the vision did not appear. After school, however, Bernadette heard an inner invitation from the lady, so she returned to the grotto and asked her again for her name, the only response being a smile. The parish priest again said: 'If the lady really wishes a chapel built, then she must tell us her name and make the rose bush bloom at the grotto.'

Thursday 4th March: the day all were waiting for

The ever-greater crowd of about 8000 people were waiting for a miracle at the end of the fortnight, but the vision was silent and the priest was sticking to his position. For 20 days, Bernadette did not go to the grotto, no longer feeling the irresistible invitation.

Thursday 25th March: the name they awaited

The vision finally revealed her name, but the wild rose bush still did not bloom. Bernadette recounted, 'She lifted her eyes up to heaven, joined her hands as though in prayer, her hands that were held out and open towards the ground, and said to me: Que soy era Immaculada Concepciou.' The young visionary left running, continuously repeating the words that she did not understand, words that troubled the brave parish priest. The uneducated Bernadette was ignorant of the fact that this theological expression had been assigned to the Blessed Virgin, Pope Pius IX having four years earlier declared this a truth of the Catholic faith, a dogma.

Wednesday 7th April: the miracle of the candle

During this apparition, Bernadette had to keep her candle alight. The candle flame licked along her hand without burning it, all witnessed by the doctor, Dr Douzous.

Thursday 16th July: the last apparition

When Bernadette received the mysterious call to the grotto, her way was blocked by a barrier so she was forced to approach the grotto from the other side of the Gave. 'I felt that I was in front of the grotto, at the same distance as before. I saw only the Blessed Virgin; never was she more beautiful.'

The rest of Bernadette's life was far from easy. She suffered continuous illness and a life of pain and hardship. In 1866, she became a nun, joining the Sisters of Nevers as Sister Marie-Bernard. Her life was spent in work, nursing and prayer. On 16th April 1879, having made her final confession and recited the Prayer of the Dying, Bernadette bent her head and died sitting in front of the fire, her last words being to ask for a drink.

Bernadette was obviously a remarkable and devoted woman, dedicated to her faith, but how does someone like this become a saint? There is no simple way for this to happen; it is a long procedure. A special religious panel is appointed, many statements and declarations are made in the name of the current Pope, the three stages towards sainthood being encompassed in a holy bond called the Congregation of Rites. Long and exhausting investigations into the goodness of the person and his or her holy devotion are made. In the case of Bernadette, the whole process lasted 24 years. There are a number of stages in this process of Beatification and Canonisation. First, on three separate occasions, Bernadette's body had to be examined – I will describe this below in some detail. After much deliberation, the stage of the Blessed was achieved in 1925, the full process of Beatification and Canonisation finally being completed when, on 8th December 1933, Pope Pius XI declared Bernadette a saint.

As I mentioned above, it was not just that Bernadette in life had to reach true holiness, but also that her body in death had to be fully intact through three examinations, and it is here that we see the importance of the physical side of death as a basis for aspects of faith. This preservation of the body is, however, not the only criterion for sainthood as obviously not all saints' bodies are 'incorruptible', i.e. intact. If they are though, this is regarded as a true sign of sainthood. It is said that the body of the Blessed Virgin Mary did not decay but, uncorrupted, was taken directly into heaven by God. This was especially important to the Christian faith as, around the time of Christ, it was Jewish tradition for the body to be laid in a tomb for approximately a year until it was fully decomposed to bones, which would then be collected by the family.

As a funeral director, I obviously also have a professional and technical interest in this area. I would love to know whether the body was embalmed or preserved in any way, but we may never be able to settle this question. The closest I have come to any reference to this is from post mortem records and the book *The Body of Saint Bernadette*, written by Father Andre Ravier. Father Ravier comments that when the wax mask of Bernadette was made, 'it was feared that although the body was mummified the blackish tinge to the face and sunken eyes and nose would make an unpleasant impression on the public'.

But is this really Bernadette's body? Surely it must have been embalmed to have survived this long? The answer, sworn on oath in the strictness of Canon law, is that it is Bernadette's body – intact – that is in the shrine and that it looks as if it has been 'mummified'. Search as I might, I have not been able to find any further reference to embalming, so did this happen or was Bernadette's mummification an act of God, in part defining her sainthood? In a previous chapter, I described the Colombian bodies apparently mummified without embalming, so it seems that anything might be possible. My faith too guides me to believe that there is something incredible surrounding the story of Bernadette's remains.

The best way forward is probably to look at the three recorded exhumations of Bernadette, called in Canon law 'the identification of the body'. Our first clue is that the nuns of Bernadette's order washed and dressed her and placed her in a coffin. After all the religious rites had been performed, she was interred in the crypt of the Chapel of Saint Joseph in the confines of the convent, interestingly in an oak shell and lead case (which would in itself have assisted in preserving her). And so began the road to sainthood for Bernadette Soubirous.

In the late summer/autumn of 1909, the early work of the commission looking into Bernadette's reputation in terms of sainthood, virtue and miracles, with a view to her Canonisation, was complete so, on Wednesday 22nd, her body was exhumed for first identification. The records from the archives of the convent, Saint Gildard, enable us to follow the identification proceedings, very correct in their formality, throughout. Monsignor Gauthey, Bishop of Nevers, and the Church Tribunal entered the main chapel of the convent at 8.30 a.m. Placed in the entrance were the Holy Gospels on a small table. The witnesses present were Abbé Perreau, Marie-Josephine Forestier, who was the Mother Superior of the Order, her deputy, Drs A. Jourdan and C.H. David, the stonemasons Gavillon and Boue, and the carpenters. An oath to tell the complete truth was signed, and all was now ready. The party, led by the Mayor and Deputy Mayor, now moved to the Chapel of Saint Joseph.

The stonemason began the work by removing the stone that made the coffin visible to all present. This was then gently removed and taken to the next room, which had been specially prepared for it. There it was placed on two trestles and covered with a plain cloth. A second table, also covered with a white cloth, was ready to receive Bernadette's remains, whether intact or just bones. The wooden coffin was then unscrewed and the inner lead coffin cut open to reveal Bernadette's body. In the words of the archive documents from the convent, 'the body was in a perfect state of preservation', those present declaring that there was not even a single trace of any unpleasant smell. The Sisters present who had buried her some 30 years earlier noted that Bernadette's hands had fallen a little to the left, but they were otherwise truly amazed at how little, if any, change had taken place. Even if the nuns had been a little biased and had seen what they wanted to see, there are also the sworn oaths of the doctors. Their report reads as follows:

The coffin was opened in the presence of the Bishop of Nevers, the Mayor of the town, his principal deputy, several Canons and ourselves. We noticed no smell. The body was clothed in the habit of Bernadette's order. The habit was damp. Only the face and forearms were uncovered.

The head was tilted to the left. The face was dull white. The skin clung to the muscles and the muscles adhered to the bones. The eyelids covered the sockets of the eyes. The brows were flat on the skin and stuck to the arches above the eyes. The lashes of the right eyelid were stuck to the skin. The nose was dilated and shrunken. The mouth was open slightly and it could been seen that the teeth were still in place. The hands, which were crossed on her breast, were perfectly preserved, as were the nails. The hands still held a rusting rosary. The veins on the forearms stood out.

Like the hands, the feet were wizened and the toenails were still intact (one of them was torn off when the corpse was washed). When the habit had been removed and the veil lifted from the head, the whole of the shrivelled body could be seen, rigid and taut in every limb.

It was found that the hair, which had been cut short, was stuck to the head and still attached to the skull – that the ears were in a state of perfect preservation – that the left side of the body was slightly higher than the right from the hip up.

The stomach had caved in and was taut like the rest of the body. It sounded like cardboard when struck.

The left knee was not as large as the right. The ribs protruded, as did the muscles in the limbs.

So rigid was the body that it could be rolled over and back for washing.

The lower parts of the body had turned slightly black. This seems to have been the result of the carbon of which large quantities were found in the coffin.

In witness of which we have duly drawn up this present statement in which all is truthfully recorded.

This perfect preservation is not necessarily miraculous. After all, it is well known that corpses decompose more slowly in certain kinds of soil and gradually mummify. The mummy named Sandy in the British Museum in London is a good example of this: whatever form of embalming he underwent at his death, it was certainly the sandy soil in which he was buried that helped to mummify him. But in Bernadette's case, the preservation is quite astounding, taking into account her illness and the state of her body when she died and the humidity in the chapel vault, as evidenced by the fact that her habit was damp, her rosary was rusty and her crucifix had turned green. So what happened? Was Bernadette's preservation the result of any form of embalming? Was it caused by the hermetic seal on the coffin? Or was Bernadette truly mummified through the will of God? It is worth noting at this point that the occurrence was, quite correctly, not considered a miracle. But whatever rare biological phenomenon might have been the scientific explanation for this, it was, in religious terms, enough to continue towards the Beatification and Canonisation of Bernadette Soubirous.

Two things then began to affect the body. First, the nuns washed it – probably not a good idea as this would later cause some deterioration. Second, having being open to the air for a number of hours, the body began to turn black. This is not unusual – I have witnessed the same after a lead coffin was opened many years after burial – as the body begins to dehydrate. At this point, Bernadette's remains were placed in a new coffin, this time lined with a strong zinc second coffin padded with silk, and again hermetically sealed and stamped with seven seals. By 5.30 p.m., all was complete, and the coffin had been returned to the vault.

In August 1913, shortly before the First World War broke out, Pope Pius X authorised the next step in the procedure by signing the Decree of Venerability; the war, however, meant that the next identification of the now Venerable Bernadette was delayed until 3rd April 1919. The second identification was undertaken by Drs Talon and Comte in the presence of the Bishop of Nevers, Monsignor Chatelus, the Police Commissioner, and members of the local government and the Church Tribunal, who were still investigating (it's not easy to become a saint!). As with the first investigation, an oath was signed and sworn, the vault was opened, and the body was removed from the coffin and reburied in the vault of St Joseph in a new coffin, all in accordance with Canon and Civil Law. The doctors retired to separate rooms to write their reports, which concurred closely. Dr Talon wrote:

There was no smell of putrefaction and none of those present experienced any discomfort. The body is practically mummified, covered with patches of mildew and quite a notable layer of salts, which appear to be calcium salts. The skeleton is complete, and it was possible to carry the body to a table without any

145

trouble. The skin has disappeared in some places, but it is still present on most parts of the body. Some of the veins are still visible.

The body had passed its second inspection.

On 18th November 1923, the Pope announced the authenticity of Bernadette's virtues and the path was open to her Beatification, one step from full Canonisation. This meant that the third identification was necessary and that the relics (various parts of the body) were to be removed and sent to Rome, Lourdes and Houses of the Order to which Bernadette belonged. As my view is that the body of a deceased person is absolutely *sacred*, I do not understand why anyone would remove parts of any departed person, let alone a saint-to-be. I would have also expected that devoted followers of the saints would regard any part of them as sacred and wish to be near them within the Church. A priest once said to me, 'Isn't it the same as keeping a baby's first teeth or a lock of hair of someone you have lost, or as in Japan where they keep the umbilical cord?' Certainly, the idea that you have to undertake surgery in death to remove these small parts does not appeal to me, however technically fascinating it might be. I expect that I just have to remember that faith is everything and that, to the Church, most relics are very precious indeed.

In tradition, relics are not necessarily parts of the body. Many relics are said to be splinters from the cross of Christ, somewhere in the Holy Land are said to be two feathers from the Holy Spirit, and much publicity surrounds the Turin Shroud, the shroud that religion (but not science) believes Christ was wrapped in before his resurrection. In Spain, it is believed that the dying breath

of St Joseph is contained in a small bottle, one enraged
cardinal once attempting to remove the cork of what he
said was a 'ridiculous illusion'. The Vatican is said to house
a 'relic bank' that holds in sacred care mementoes of many
saints. This means that if a new Church of St Bernadette,
for example, were opened, a piece of her liver or a splinter
of rib could be sent to be placed in the altar there for all to
see.

My views on relics aside, the third, most important and
final identification of the body took place on 18th April
1925, 46 years after Bernadette's death. Drs Talon and
Comte were once again asked to examine the body, and
surgeon Dr Comte was assigned the unpleasant task
of removing the relics. In line with requirements, the
ceremony was held in private, with priests, nuns, the
Bishop, the vicars-general, the Church Tribunal, two
'instrumental' witnesses, the two doctors, the Police
Commissioner and Leon Bruneton from the municipal
authorities present, as well as undertakers, masons,
carpenters and other workmen. 'I swear and promise to
faithfully accomplish the task with which I have been
entrusted', declared the doctors, 'and to tell the truth in
the replies I make to questions put to me and in my
written statements on the examination of the Venerable
Servant of God, Sister Marie-Bernard Soubirous, and on
the removal of the relics. This, I promise and swear. So
help me God and the Holy Gospels.' Each of the workmen
took an oath: 'With my hand on God's Gospels I swear
and promise to faithfully accomplish the task with which
I have been entrusted. So help me God and the Holy
Gospels.'

The coffin was carried in procession to the chapel of

St Helen for the investigations. Here are some passages from Dr Comte's report:

At the request of the Bishop of Nevers I detached and removed the rear section of the fifth and sixth ribs as relics; I noted that there was a resistance, hard mass in the thorax; which was the liver covered by the diaphragm. I also took a piece of the diaphragm and the liver beneath it as relics, and can affirm that this organ was in a remarkable state of preservation. I also removed the two patella bones to which the skin clung and which were covered with more clinging calcium matter.

Finally I removed the muscle fragments right and left from the outsides of the thighs. These muscles were also in a very good state of preservation and did not seem to have putrefied at all. From this examination I conclude that the body of the Venerable Bernadette is intact, the skeleton is complete, the muscles have atrophied, but are very well preserved; only the skin, which has shrivelled, seems to have suffered from the effects of the damp in the coffin. It has taken on a greyish tinge and is covered with patches of mildew and quite a large number of crystals and calcium salts; but the body does not seem to have putrefied, nor has any decomposition of the cadaver set in, although this would be expected and normal after such a long period in a vault hollowed out of the earth.

Three years later, in 1928, Dr Comte published a 'report on the exhumation of the Blessed Bernadette' in the second issue of the *Bulletin de l'Association médicale de Notre-Dame de Lourdes*. 'I would have liked', he wrote, 'to open the left side of the thorax to take the ribs as relics and then remove the heart which I am certain must have survived; however, as the trunk was slightly supported on the left arm, it would have been rather difficult to try and get at the heart without doing too much noticeable damage. As the Mother Superior had expressed a desire for the Saint's heart to be kept together with the whole body, and as Monsignor the Bishop did not insist, I gave up the idea of opening the left-hand side of the thorax and contented myself with removing the two right ribs which were more accessible.'

The surgeon was particularly impressed by the state of preservation of the liver: 'what struck me during this examination, of course, was the state of perfect preservation of the skeleton, the fibrous tissues of the muscles (still supple and firm), of the ligaments and of the skin, and above all the totally unexpected state of the liver after 46 years. One would have thought that this organ, which is basically soft and inclined to crumble, would have decomposed very rapidly or would have hardened to a chalky consistency. Yet when it was cut it was soft and almost normal in consistency. I pointed this out to those present, remarking that this did not seem to be a natural phenomenon.'

Bernadette was now, deservedly, accorded sainthood, her body being on view at Nevers. It is all too easy to forget that our ways of dealing with death can help to construct our faith just as much as our personal faith, whatever it is, supports us through these difficult times. Bernadette represents the epitome of goodness and faith in the Catholic Church. Millions of individuals have witnessed a change in our lives brought about through a simple child, a catalyst, which brings so many of us in procession to Lourdes. It seems that someone like Bernadette, who brought so much to the world in life, with faith, brings so much more in death. Being a saint carries so much responsibility! It is interesting to remember too that, at a time when respect for the dead brings repose of the soul and peace, Bernadette was promised happiness not in this life but the next.

9

East meets West

'The Virtuoso' – well, there's something I've never been described as (although I have been described as many things before now!), but that is the term used to describe a funeral director in Japan. I once watched a specially made video that had been produced by the Japanese funeral industry to promote the Japanese funeral service. It started with some beautiful classical music played by a violin virtuoso, underlining the fact that a virtuoso is a leader, a master. It then went on to compare the two 'artists'. The funeral director is, it claimed, the first stop, the one who guides and shows the bereaved the way forward; the musical virtuoso is likewise followed by his colleagues. To me, however, the conductor is the one in charge of the orchestra, and, in a similar way, we describe the person in charge of the funeral as the conductor. 'Good morning Madam, I'm the Virtuoso; I've come to virtuoso the funeral today.' No, I think I'll stick to my description. But, that aside, the video was professionally arranged and very informative.

As a young man growing up in the funeral business, I often commented that we had never conducted the funeral of a Japanese person. In 40 years, we had neither cremated nor repatriated even one person from Japan. Were there so many Japanese around because they never died?! We had undertaken funerals for all religions and nationalities yet it was not until April 2000 that we had a Japanese client, and then the following year, we dealt with six more, quite unconnected, funerals for Japanese people. Life is very strange indeed.

In spring 2002, just months before football's World Cup, I attended the Fédération Internationale des Associations de Thanatologues/International Federation of Thanatologists Associations (FIAT/IFTA) World Conference in Kyoto, the old capital of Japan, as UK delegate on behalf of the UK funeral industry. Over 500 people attended, representing 29 countries worldwide. We were in Japan because the Japanese delegate was President of the organisation. At this same meeting, I was to be elected as a Vice President, to become President (all being well) in 2006 at Beijing in China. The ceremony for the new President and Vice President was very grand and formal, just what you would expect: many gifts, lots of bowing and very complimentary introductions. Sitting in my seat in the large circle, with the Union Jack, a microphone and an earphone for translation, I felt as if I were at the United Nations or one of the *Four Just Men*, a programme from the early 1960s that I would stay up late and watch with my Nan on a Saturday night.

I was to give a speech from the main stage for a period of not more than one hour and not less than one hour (very precise, the Japanese). I was to speak about cryonics and the funeral service. The first three speakers were German, Chinese and Korean respectively, and in their speeches – of *precisely* an hour's duration – there was not one joke or giggle. Mine, needless to say, was to open with a little light-hearted humour. As I approached the stage, facing 500 or more international members and around 500 other day attendants, I was very, very nervous. I was clapped as I mounted the stage, but then total polite silence fell. With the immortal words from the television series *Star Trek* 'Beam me up, Scotty!' – flashing through my head, I began with 'Good afternoon' in English and Japanese. I looked up. Not even a smile for effort. I followed up with 'I wrote this speech very slowly because I don't read very fast.' I looked up again, this time to what could only be described in common (very common) cockney as 'a thousand faces like smacked arses'. But just as I looked down, I heard a huge flurry of laughter echoing around the hall, and it was then I realised that they were simply waiting for the translation system to kick in. 'Yes,' I thought, 'you've cracked it, Barry!'

Considering that this was a meeting mainly of under-takers, the following 59 minutes went with much jollity: if the truth be told, undertakers really are a good-humoured lot. 'What does an undertaker wear at a wedding, a party or a funeral? – black of course', as my old Dad would say; good for all occasions. I finished on time and to a polite standing round of applause; I too was presented with gifts and subjected to an endless stream of camera clicks, many of the photographs being sent on to me later in the year.

One reason I was being placed in the limelight was that, in the year preceding the conference, I had been developing and producing a new international travel pass for the dead.

There is a passport for the living, so why not for the dead? This 'International Transportation Document for the Dead' contains 56 pages with a translation in 26 languages. The items are linked by number; if, for example, human remains were being transported from England to Brazil via France, the UK funeral director would complete the section in English on page 3 and link it with the French translation on page 5 and the Portuguese translation on page 15. When the remains arrive in France, anyone can check the details in number order by turning to the French section; similarly, the Portuguese section will be consulted when the remains arrive in Brazil. In the front of the document is a pouch to contain the legal documents necessary for international repatriation. I am proud to say that this has been accepted with great enthusiasm, has been purchased around the world and is now in regular use.

So, anyway, there I was in Japan, with much to see and at least one final departure to follow as the group of delegates were lucky enough to be taken on a number of field visits. Everything in Japan, including funerals, is very expensive. The funeral homes in Kyoto are like office blocks: the vehicles are on the first floor (what we in the UK would call the ground floor), the chapel on the second, the service room on the third, storage on the fourth, offices on the fifth and so on. Very few people are buried in Japan: there is no room, there is little demand and the cost of land for burial is just too high for most people.

Most of the services in Japan are Buddhist cremations, and we were honoured to be able to witness such a service from beginning to end. It was a very formal service of worship, respect and much burning of incense. It also seems that some days are considered good for cremation and some bad. The Buddhist altar is very special and valuable, made by craftsmen with much religious love and care. The body is placed in a simple, casket-shaped box and dressed as tradition demands. It is not, however, central in the same way as it is in cultures such as the Italian or Irish.

After the final viewing, the deceased is taken in a special hearse to the crematorium. These 'special' hearses are unique and, to Western eyes, somewhat strange. They are, in many cases, Nissan pick-up trucks with beautifully carved wooden Buddhist canopies, each specially prepared, religiously blessed and consecrated in accordance with the Buddhist faith. I made extensive enquiries through the interpreter, who confirmed the cost of one such vehicle at around £100,000. Yes, £100,000. Nowadays, a Nissan pick-up truck is around £14,000 in the UK and a suitable wooden canopy another £14,000. I have to admit the businessman in me was thinking, well, I could get the canopy made for around £5000 in Spain and import it, maybe £19,000 all in, a nice little earner! – but what I was of course missing was the Buddhist love, care and special blessings that are handcrafted into each one. In addition, each canopy is completely unique in its artistry.

The importance of cremation to the Japanese can be seen by a brief look at some statistics. In the year 2000, there were over 7000 crematoriums in Japan, of which only approximately 1600 were conducting one or more cremations a year and were operating with the three basic elements: a building, a cremator and air exhaustion equipment. Most of the remaining crematoriums were open-field ones, cremation being conducted with natural materials. Approximately 30 facilities were newly built in 2001. Of the 1,005,211 deaths in 2000, over 99% per cent of bodies underwent cremation, figures very similar to those for 1999.

Let's compare that with Great Britain, with only 243 crematoriums. Using provisional figures for 2001, about 71% of the approximately 640,000 deaths went to cremation, still a very high figure and around the same value as for 2000. The Republic of Ireland, however, is still very against cremation, and has only three crematoriums, the latest being opened in 2001 in Dublin. Here, only 5.4 per cent of an estimated 32,000 deceased people were cremated in 2001 (from 5.65 per cent in 2000), and there is no national cremation society. This is in complete contrast to Japan, and the picture is equally variable and unpredictable around the world (see the appendix at the end of the chapter). Fewer than 10 per cent of people undergo cremation in countries such as Argentina, Cuba (a tiny 0.47 per cent), Ghana and Italy, countries such as the Czech Republic, Denmark, Hong Kong and Switzerland having a figure of over 70 per cent. In between lie, for example, France (19 per cent), Austria (21 per cent), the Peoples Republic of China (47 per cent) and Sweden (69 per cent).

The crematorium that I visited in Kyoto was set on a hill overlooking the city. We entered a building that was a little like a cinema or theatre; this was where the service was to take place and the tributes of respect paid. The coffin was then removed, the close family escorting it to the building that contained 23 cremation ovens. In the UK, most crematoriums have about three or four cremators so that gives you an idea of the size of this place. Here, the family said their final goodbyes, and the head of the family pushed the button to ignite the flames. They all then went upstairs to a lounge where they enjoyed the Japanese speciality of green tea. The superintendent of the crematorium, a very smart man truly proud of his position and his crematorium, who had taken some 40 years to achieve his high status of 'protector', returned to the lounge several hours later. He reported to the funeral director that the flame was now extinguished and the family could proceed to the Room of Bones (the ashes room). Here, the main mourners, the important members of the family, chose a piece of the deceased and placed it in the small urn for safe-keeping. These urns and their contents would then be handed down through the generations.

What was left was then placed in the hills around the crematorium, to be reunited with their ancestors, the Japanese being very proud of their ancestral past. The small pieces of bones were still really hot while they were being collected with small sticks (like chopsticks). This was a very proud moment for the family, full of controlled emotion but completed without tears or fear. I could not imagine a British family being able to cope with such a task. Having to see, only hours after the funeral, the cremated remains of a relative straight from the oven would be neither acceptable or manageable for us.

This highlights the comfort that following our own traditions can give. Such traditions are inbred, almost in the blood. Only true traditions that come from deep inside, that are passed on from generation to generation, can truly be called tradition. Tradition is the backbone of Japanese life, and in death it is of no lesser importance. Placing the remainder of the bones in the hillside is very different too from British practice. In the UK, even the smaller pieces of ash are kept together, the family being left with the choice afterwards of what they do with them. I have known people to separate and scatter them in many different places; it is a very personal thing. In contrast, Japanese culture seems in some ways to sacrifice individual choice to produce a loving and respectful chain to the past and future that all are reluctant to break. What we need to remember though is that whatever our culture, tradition or final resting place, losing a loved one is equally painful to all.

This issue of accepted practices arose again when I hosted a Chinese delegation in my own funeral home in London. The delegation consisted of funeral workers and managers through to government ministers and military people, all exceptionally serious but, just like my Japanese colleagues, very respectful. After a tour of the premises and an Albin's Catering lunch, I gave a talk about the British funeral service, at the end of which I asked whether there were any questions. Like the Japanese, these delegates had a problem with choice but, unlike the Japanese, they had no under-standing of freedom – freedom to choose, freedom from government interference. Every question was about legisla-tion, government requirements, what the government would allow. Did the government employ me? Did the government own Albin's? (No, the bank and the tax man, I was tempted to retort.) Could they have a list of government cremation rules? Could they see the govern-ment's burial rules? Every question and every enquiry related to government approval.

The interpreter explained that all these people had, in truth, been brought up not only by their families, but also by the government. She believed that a change in the people's liberty would come about very slowly in China, partly because the government would restrict it but also because most of the people would at first resist it. Like traditions, some opinions are passed on from generation to generation, and it may not be possible for China to modernise overnight. Change will, however, come through travel and long-term education. But is change necessary? Sometimes, I believe, but not always. Although freedom and liberty are, to me, the foundation of life and should always be striven for, some traditions are quite beautiful in their simplicity and should be kept as such.

The Chinese group, now well fed and educated on the British funeral service, as well as equipped with a thousand photographs, went on to their next stop in Germany. As I wished them 'Auf wiedersehen', I could not help thinking 'Yes, we will meet again'. On my trip to the East, I had met Mr Fan Zliaoqi, the President of the Chinese Funeral Service and Government Minister for Death, in Beijing, China. What I found strange here was the lack of interest in the history of the funeral service. In my talk in London, I had given much information about the company's history, albeit with very little response, and I now realised that the Chinese interest was only of a practical nature and functions in conjunction with their communist state.

Chinese final departures are a very public affair with very little individuality or privacy. Most surprising to me was the incredible technical ability inherent in their cremation procedures, showing almost clockwork precision. Cremation, made official in China only in 1956, occurs mainly in the big cities – Beijing, Shanghai, Tianjin, Liaoning, Jiling, Heilongjiang, Shandong – where the cremation rate is about 90 per cent compared with a national rate of around 47 per cent. From this, it does not take a degree in maths to work out that 53 per cent of the population nationally are still buried. There is of course plenty of space in China for burial, and in some parts of China the wood fuel that is required for cremation is itself in short supply and precious.

A huge and incredible crematorium was recently built in Beijing, designed like a space station and cremating around 300 people each day. When you think that a large crematorium in the UK may well cremate up to 30 people on a busy day, the logistics are remarkable. The crematorium is laid out in what can only be described as a massive circle. Unlike the UK, where funeral homes are separate from crematoriums, the two are combined in China, fully state run and with state-of-the-art (perhaps a little too much so for me) technology.

The case which was demonstrated was that of a middle-aged man whose family had arranged the funeral two days before. They arrived at the crematorium for the appointed time of 10 a.m., along with the 30 other families attending funerals that were to take place in the building at this same time. It was very crowded and noisy, a kind of organised chaos, and I had to remember that there is very little privacy in China. The cremation number was 49 so the family went to service room 49 for a Buddhist service lasting only minutes before being hurried upstairs to viewing hall 49. Meanwhile the coffin and the deceased were moved, on a golf cart, to a conveyor belt, which transported the deceased along to bay 49 (again the magic number). What happened next was, to me, very unusual. The coffin lid was removed by a robot-like arm and replaced by a glass lid, the whole process being fully automated. The body, now fully displayed under the glass, was lifted onto a platform and up into bay 49 where the family was waiting to grieve and wave goodbye for the last time. It was certainly

bizarre to see the open-top coffin rising from the ground –
all too automated and impersonal for me. The glass top
was finally removed, to be used again for the 11.00 funeral.

The coffin was replaced on the cart and removed to
cremator 49 for the cremation, the family waiting in the
communal lounge until the cremation had been completed.
They were then invited to divide the ashes and bones as
they saw fit. Where? – in room 49 of course. Every
cremation is exactly the same – no choice, no personal
contribution, seemingly no true connection with tradition
or personal values. Even the name seemed important only
as a check that the right body was being dealt with.

Unlike the Japanese, who cling rigidly to tradition, the
Chinese government makes every effort to change tradition
and simple procedures. There are constant reforms in
Chinese society, the most recent being in 1997 when a
directive was given to the people to change funeral customs.
In the government's words, 'The deepening processing
reform of funeral customs is mainly setting a civilised
and new prevailing practise in funeral service.' I will quote
here the new rules (in their not entirely perfect English
translation in *The Brief Introduction on the Chinese Funeral
Situation*):

1. paying last respects to the remains of the dead instead
   of informing relatives and friends of a death and
   taking part in the funeral procession;
2. laying a wreath to the remains of the dead instead of
   burning joss sticks and laying offerings before the
   dead;
3. wearing black gauze and white paper flower instead of
   putting on mourning;

4. making a deep bow and standing in silent tribute instead of kneeling and touching the ground with the forehead, worshipping on knees;
5. playing funeral music in lieu of beating drums, blowing trumpets and firing firecrackers.

Two new funeral methods are also being promoted in the directives: scattering ashes over the sea and planting trees on ashes sites in large and medium-sized cities. This is moving towards not preserving the ashes, whereas they were previously kept as a keepsake for the family – a big change. This approach seems to be being accepted more readily in urban than rural areas.

The Chinese funeral service is nationalised like no other anywhere in the world: the government has a total monopoly even over repatriation:

China International Transport Corpse Network Service Centre of China Funeral Association is a sole associated service organisation authorised by the State to manage international transport remains business. In accordance with the relative regulations of the State, the international transport remains must be carried out uniform channel to the appropriate department for management. All transport remains from leaving China's territory or arriving at China's territory and all funeral activities within the boundary of China must be undertaken uniformly only by China International Transport Corpse Network Service Centre of China Funeral Association and its designated funeral homes at the local levels. Any other departments including any insurance or agencies established in

China by foreigners will not do to undertake this kind of business without authorisation.

So a company like mine could not operate a repatriation service even if we were being asked to deal with someone who had died in China, and the government repatriation service is not cheap. Having said that, the Chinese gift for 'copying' or 'replicating' means that they have the ability to take, for example, a removal trolley or stretcher made in the US and copy it *to perfection* at half the price. But even though procedure can be copied, a high standard, privacy and freedom to choose cannot be duplicated. For this to happen, you must change the way you think and not just pay lip service to a new approach. All in all though, I have been very surprised by the recent progress I have seen in Chinese funeral practice – long may it continue.

Somewhere between the extremes of the totally traditional and the totally modern lies the most interesting and simple funeral practice I have observed, that of a Korean nation wishing to promote itself as modern and caring, yet steeped in tradition and honour. The video presentation I was privileged to attend opened with a beautiful final departure. On the side of a hill, a traditional Buddhist shrine or bier was being carried by no less than 12 men, the body of the deceased lying uncovered on top. These men wore traditional clothing of white hoods and gowns, and their procession was accompanied by drum-beating and much chanting. For the first few minutes, I was completely moved by this: how different from the Japanese and Chinese promotions. It seemed so old and authentic. What I had not expected was the fact that this journey up the hill was to last for some 30 minutes on the video, each minute being exactly the same as the one before. It was a record of the whole final trip up the hill to the funeral pyre, and I could only marvel at the fortitude of the pall-bearers.

Then, about 32 minutes into the upward struggle, and just as I was beginning to feel my eyes closing, the camera travelled for the first time to the feet of the monks or bearers – to show not the expected bare feet or sandals but matching white and black Nike trainers. And not only that, but the men were also wearing shorts and white socks, so there was a gap between the bottom of the gown and the top of the socks, showing a row of little white legs resembling milk bottles. All this wonderful tradition and authentic costume and then, right at the end, post-millennium commercialisation breaks through. My colleagues from around the world and I struggled as we were overtaken by the funny side of how the filming of such a sincere cremation rite had been undermined by this rather out-of-place set of images. The video ended at the top of the hill, where, in rural Korean style, the body was cremated in the open, the traditional again holding sway. Interestingly, there are no statistics on cremation for either North or South Korea, as if they want to be part of the rest of the world without fully joining in.

My last encounter in the East was with a bright and funny young man from Vietnam, who followed me all over the Chinese convention. Mr Phoung Phoung ran a repatriation and funeral service in Hanoi and spoke good English, albeit with a highly American accent. He knew my connections with the Kenyon Repatriation Service and was very keen to become our agent in Vietnam. He insisted on taking us out for a drink so we found ourselves in a beer bar sitting, as is customary, on the floor with a Budweiser beer and snacks – not your usual crisps or nuts but pickled octopus and squid, looking for all the world as if they had been swimming just moments earlier. Mr Phoung Phoung had much delight in swallowing a small squid whole, licking his lips and encouraging myself and Jackie to take the plunge. Jackie, without a second thought, ate hers and smiled at me, knowing I was next to go. She already knew from Anita, the FIAT/IFTA secretary, that I really disliked such food but also knew I could not escape the delicacy. Closing my eyes and taking the smallest piece possible, I swallowed it in one gulp. Laughter rang out from my Vietnamese colleague and he said, 'You thought you would offend me, didn't you?' 'Yes', I replied. 'No way,' he chuckled 'let's get a beer.' I'd been had.

Needless to say, we got on really well after that and he duly became our agent in Vietnam, promising me I would not regret it. At that point I doubted we would ever have any work from Vietnam, but how wrong I was! Since then, he has sent us 10 cases, the lesson here obviously being that no matter how small the business seems, it is never a good idea to turn your nose up at it. In Eastern philosophical terms, everything has a small beginning. There may be just one drop of water, but that single drop mingles with another and trickles down to join other drops until it becomes a puddle. It may then gently flow into a small stream, running on into a river and then an ocean, now being part of something very powerful.

It feels to me that Vietnam may be showing the greatest will for freedom of all the Eastern nations I have seen – not what anyone would have thought back in the 1960s. As most of the deceased persons repatriated to us from

Vietnam were on holiday when they died, the borders are certainly opening up. The Vietnamese were not secretive about their cremation statistics but unfortunately did not have any; all they could tell me was that they had only two crematoriums in the country. Fair enough, I suppose; I'm sure nobody minds waiting their turn. But what a great contact I have there. Working with death does not mean you cannot be full of life, you know!

Cremation statistics

Country	Number of crematoriums	Cremations 2000	Cremations 2001	Percentage of deaths
Argentina	42	**14,652	**16,632	7.53
Australia	74	No information available		
Austria	11	16,663	16,048	21.46
Belgium	10	35,798	36,678	*35.17
Brazil (São Paulo only)	4	No information available		
Canada	143	No information available		
China, People's Republic of	1420	3,737,000	3,781,000	47.30
Colombia	17	No information available		
Confederation of Independent States	8	No information available		
Cuba (Havana City only)	1	69	89	0.47
Czech Republic	27	82,772	81,940	76.04
Denmark	32	41,651	41,707	71.30
Finland	20	13,037	13,391	27.58
France	98	93,412	100,238	18.91
Germany	120	No information available		
Ghana	4	300	334	1.78

Country	Number of crematoriums	Cremations 2000	Cremations 2001	Percentage of deaths
Great Britain	243	437,609	427,994	*70.70
Haiti	1	268	245	N/A
Hong Kong	12	27,113	26,893	80.75
Hungary	10	44,714	43,784	33.68
Iceland	1	212	234	13.60
Ireland, Republic of	3	1759	**1728	**5.40
Italy	36	29,783	36,031	6.62
Japan	1630	999,255	No information available	
Latvia	1	1127	1297	12.39
Luxembourg	1	No information available		
Namibia	1	231	217	N/A
Netherlands, The	57	68,700	69,039	49.22
New Zealand	31	No information available		
Norway	40	14,039	14,114	32.03
Peru (Lima only)	3	No information available		
Portugal (Lisbon only)	2	1544	1765	19.58
Romania (Bucharest only)	2	No information available		
Slovenia, Republic of (Ljubljana only)	2	7085	7823	42.40
South Africa	32	31,836	33,427	**6.00
Spain	83	48,689	53,694	14.92
Sweden	69	64,867	65,223	69.57
Switzerland	27	45,104	45,681	75.51
Trinidad & Tobago	3	365	No information available	
US	1711	630,800	*653,350	*27.12
Zimbabwe (Harare only)	2	840	No information available	

* Provisional figures ** Estimated figures

10

The immortalists

Cryonics seems to provide the only alternative to burial and cremation we have, but why should I choose this method and why, even then, should I want to join the Cryonics Institute (CI), based in Michigan? Let the CI tell you in its own words.

1. **Membership qualifies you to arrange and fund a full-body cryopreservation:** treatment and cooling upon legal death, followed by long-term storage in liquid nitrogen. Instead of certain death, you and your loved ones could have a chance at eventual healthy physical revival.
2. **The most affordable suspension prices.** CI offers full body suspensions that begin at $28,000 – tens of thousands of dollars less than other organisations.
3. **The most affordable membership prices.** Become an Option One member and you have a

secure membership for life, all for a one-time payment of only $1250, and no mandatory dues to pay, ever again. Join under Option Two and there's no joining fee, and dues are only $120 a year – less than the cost of a cable TV subscription!

4. **Lower prices for spouses and children.** Are you an Option One member? Then the cost of Option One membership for your spouse is half-price. And minor children receive membership absolutely free.

5. **Quality of treatment.** CI is the **only** cryonics organisation that has a Ph.D. level cryobiologist with over twenty years' experience as its Director of Research. CI has a separate laboratory near its main facility, engaged full time in developing improved procedures, and CI alone has its experimental results tested at independent universities and labs.

6. **Fast response time.** CI's use of local surgically trained morticians means members get knowledgeable licensed care as quickly as possible, minimising long, damaging waits till distant teams arrive.

7. **Funding through life insurance.** We generally accept European and non-U.S. life insurance policies also. Other payment methods are also available, payment usually not required until death.

8. **Free informational and other benefits.** Members have access to CI's award-winning web site at **www.cryonics.org,** and to our free e-newsletter and upcoming benefits like informational CDs and ebooks.

9. **Free ongoing DNA sample storage.** After buying

a $49 sampling kit and paying $49 for shipping and handling, CI stores tissue samples as long as desired at no further charge, absolutely free – whether from members, their families, or pets.

10. **Support for research and education.** Membership fees give you the right – though not the obligation – to execute a contract for cryonic suspension. But it also helps fund cryobiological research, educate and inform the public, and advance perhaps the most significant health care idea ever conceived.

The choice is simple. Irreversible physical death, dissolution, and decay, or a possible second chance at a vibrant, joyful life. Do you want that chance for yourself, your spouse, your parents, your children, and the people you love? For humanity as a whole?

Join us. Choose life.

The Cryonics Institute's 43rd human whole body patient died of Cancer in Toronto Canada at home under Hospice care. After professional perfusion (that's what we also do here pre-freezing), the Patient [note the Institute's use of the word 'patient' here, a denial of final death] arrived this December at the Cryonics Institute in Michigan, Detroit, U.S.A. The freezing process has now been completed and the Patient is settled in a newly complete Cryostat.

That's how someone like me hears about any new CI cases – hot off the fax machine and e-mail in brochures and press releases. But we still don't know what cryonics really is. Here is how it is described by David Pascal, a fine gentleman from the CI's PR department.

Cryonics and the future of Mortuary Service

You've almost certainly heard of cryonics. Between films like *Vanilla Sky* and news of sports great Ted Williams' suspension, the idea's become part of modern life. People are frozen expecting that future technology can fix the physical damage that caused their death, and the freezing damage that accompanies suspension. And be restored to life.

You may even know that cryonics is making the transition from science fiction to science fact. The Cryonics Institute web site at www.cryonics.org has pages of positive evaluations from PhDs, MDs, scientists, who not only publicly support cryonics but have even signed up for the process themselves.

But what you might not know is why cryonics matters to the mortician and the mortuary industry. And why cryonics could one day completely transform the practice of both.

Why Morticians?
Morticians [undertakers] have been used in cryonics from the very beginning. But not without controversy. And that's because cryonics has two problems – to which morticians may be the best solution.

The first problem is that people, who want cryonics procedures performed, need competent and legal surgical treatment. When a person dies, cryonics mandates that the person's blood – much like in embalming – is replaced with a preservative solution called a cryoprotectant that serves as an 'anti-freeze'. Without it, far more ice crystals form, and tremendous (though arguably repairable) damage is the result.

The second problem is that this procedure, and cooling itself, has to be done as quickly as possible after death. The longer a deceased person remains at room temperature, the greater the damage and decay.

The surgical skills, the proximity, the professionalism of morticians made them an ideal choice to apply cryonics procedures. But in the 1970's, there was a call in some quarters for 'medical model' suspensions. Morticians, it was said, were not medical personnel and did not 'look medical enough'.

The suggested alternative was Remote Standby Teams – groups surgically trained in cryonics procedures, who would assemble, collect their equipment, and fly to a member's bedside in a crisis.

Fine in theory, this often proved disastrous in practice. A patient might die and hours if not days pass before the team might be assembled and arrived. Surgical training in an embalming-like procedure for a few days a year, on dummies, could never approach a mortician's long expertise. Costs mushroomed as the standby team often charged thousands per day simply to wait by the member's bedside. Who sometimes was so uncooperative as to actually recover and live!

A split developed, with one of the major cryonics organisations using Standby Teams despite the practical demerits. The other – the Cryonics Institute, founded by mathematics and physics professor Robert Ettinger, the 'father of cryonics' and author of *The Prospect Of*

Immortality – opted to integrally incorporate morticians into the cryonics process.

What is the process?

What does a mortician 'do' when working with the Cryonics Institute? First, a person interested in cryonics joins CI, and arranges to fund the suspension. (Through life insurance if you wish).

CI encourages the member to then find and select a local mortician directly. The personal contact gives the member better knowledge about the mortician's technical experience and qualifications and increases confidence. The member arranges to pay the mortician separately for his services.

CI then sends the mortician a set of basic procedural instructions. Further questions are answered via phone or email with CI, and through our principal morticians (funeral director James Walsh of Michigan, in the US, and Barry Albin of Albin & Sons, in Europe), till the mortician has a thorough understanding of the process.

CI sends the mortician the necessary solutions. (And additional equipment, if the member requests and funds it – a CPR unit, for instance).

Once everything is ready, the waiting begins. CI members have ID bracelets or necklaces stating what to do in the event of death. Upon dying, or when death is imminent, CI headquarters is instantly contacted. CI HQ contacts the mortician. The mortician goes immediately to the member. Once the member dies, or if the member has already died, the mortician waits for death to be legally pronounced and registered, cools the head instantly, generally with bags of ice, and removes the member to the mortuary facilities.

There – depending on the patient's condition – the suspension procedure is performed. Arrangements are made to fly the patient packed in ice in a hermetically sealed Zeigler box to CI headquarters. CI also requires a full detailed report of the procedure and the mortician's observations to be made upon a video if possible.

Finally the patient arrives at CI where he or she is cooled to minus 196 degrees Centigrade but very slowly. First in a dry ice container which takes the person down to minus 80 degrees Centigrade, then into a temporary cryostat until minus 196 degrees Centigrade is reached. The patient is then transferred to a permanent cryostat, upside down, until such time that science may provide for defrosting.

How does Cryonics differ from embalming?
How does the cryonics process differ from standard embalming practice? In few respects, really. But the most critical are time and (perhaps) attitude.

Morticians are used to thinking of their subjects as being irrevocably dead. CI, its members and their families and supportive friends do not agree. CI does not ask that morticians share their beliefs, but it does ask that they understand that the dead they treat are considered to be certain heart attack or drowning victims – non-living, but restorable, and in desperate need of rapid care.

Morticians must reach and treat dying or deceased members *rapidly.* A mortician cannot leave the patient at room temperature, while he takes a personal call or a break. Great, discernible, and perhaps irrecoverable damage may result.

Also, the mortician is needed for surgical expertise. Mortuary practice is in no small part a consoling and legal-paperwork, but in the course of actual treatment, morticians should not see themselves as someone treating a dead body, but rather as surgically trained specialists using medical-level skills upon a patient whose life and health are critically dependent upon them. Air bubbles must not be allowed while perfusing, for instance – the internal damage may not be visible, but may be vast. And internal damage is the central consideration. Cosmetics is not: CI does not care how the patient looks or smells. The goal is to keep the patient's brain in as close to the condition it was at the moment of death as possible.

Why do it?

Because it's interesting. Morticians are not surgeons, but they are intelligent individuals with extensive surgical training and an extraordinary depth of experience. CI has often been told that the freshness and rigor of cryonics procedure is a fascinating break from standard workaday practice. Morticians find that in treating cryonics members like patients, they treat themselves to the roles of doctor and they enjoy the challenge and respect of that role.

And then there is the pleasure of perhaps, just perhaps, actually saving lives, rather than graciously concluding them. Death and bereavement are, when all is said and done, painful horrors. The prospect of using one's skill to perhaps save lives brings a new and exhilarating perspective. To console the bereaved is a compassionate thing; but to be thanked by the deceased's family for perhaps *saving* their lives, to be a bringer of hope rather than consolation, has been one of the greatest surprises our morticians have experienced. And one of the most satisfying.

Are we entering then a new era where morticians are seen, not as concluding a person's life, but rather as saving it? An era where cryonics may be restoring life not only to patients but to the mortuary industry as well?

We are.

So you now have a better idea – straight from the horse's mouth – of what cryonics is all about, although I have a feeling that saving life like this would actually bring about the demise of the funeral industry! It must be remembered here though that cryonics is a form of life extension and not a way to life ever after.

Although I would never want cryopreservation for myself, I have worked with the CI for over 10 years. It is a non-profit-making organisation that is debt free and run by a very respectable group of sincere people. I occasionally joke a little about my role in cryonics perfusion, but these people are fun people, deadly serious about their cryonics science, but real fun, even if a trifle extrovert. They say things like 'Why be cryonically suspended?' – 'Well, dead people don't have much fun, do they?' 'Why spend such a sum of money on cryonics?' – 'You can't take it with you, and there are no pockets in shrouds' (an old chestnut, that one). 'What if you come back and don't like it?' – 'Well, if we don't like it, we won't stay, will we?' 'What will you live on when and if you return?' – 'Ah, we've thought of that one and put money into a trust fund in Liechtenstein.' Truly, cryonics is not *ever* for me: one life on this earth is enough, thanks very much. But many people do believe in it, and since I became involved with cryonics, science seems to have gone mad. Various cryonicists have related to me the following advances, which they believe will lead up to the first defrosting of a 'patient'.

We are all now used to medical advances that would have been unthought of even 50 years ago. The transplantation of vital organs is commonplace today, whereas in the 1960s it was merely science fiction. During open-heart surgery, the human heart is stopped and suspended for a time before being repaired and then restarted. This is now an accepted and regular procedure during surgery, those who have undergone such a revival leading completely normal lives and retaining all their memory. Over the past 10 years, developments in DNA testing have changed the world for ever, and we are used to hearing about children – quite normal and well adjusted – who have been born from frozen embryos.

Some reports seem a bit more outlandish, but who knows what they will lead to. Human ears have been grown on the backs of mice, in the hope that such ears will one day be transplanted to humans. In the same way, human kidneys are being grown in pigs, to be transplanted to kidney disease sufferers. Dolly the Sheep hit the headlines as the first sheep to be successfully cloned, and a religious group based in the US has claimed to have cloned two human babies, although there is still some debate over this.

All this leads on to research into cryonics. Much

work has been carried out in Russia, and many developments in the use of new drugs have come from the study of cryonics and memory retention. I am sure it may be feasible for Alzheimer's and Parkinson's diseases, for example, to benefit from such developments in the future; the CI spends a lot of time and money investigating such possibilities. There have been claims that hamsters have been frozen and revived. They have been reported to have lived a normal life and, most importantly, retained their memory, although we have no way of knowing the underlying effect that this might have had on them. Even NASA, the US National Aeuronautics and Space Administration programme, is said to be experimenting with cryonics for future space travel, and I would suspect that far more extreme and frightening experiments than those described here are taking place somewhere in the world.

Resuscitation after a short period of death is even now a daily event, and I think that, perhaps one day in the distant future, scientists and doctors will find a way to repair complicated body parts and maybe even a way to revive people after longer periods of being dead. Defrosting and 'resurrecting' people is, however, a very different matter. I am quite happy to believe that an arm or a leg can work again, but what I cannot and will not accept is the retention of memory, personality or character. I believe, you see, in the soul, that unique thing that makes us different from each other, the one thing that science cannot touch and cannot explain.

The soul of a person is, I believe, real and precious in life, and death brings a change; indeed, I often refer to a kind of aura around a dead person. It is of course impossible to define this completely, but when you work with the dead as closely as I do, you get to appreciate that special soulfulness that often surrounds death, especially at the moment of death itself. Perhaps the removal of pain brings with it a kind of peacefulness. Have you ever met someone and thought that this is a remarkable person, a person full of life, an 'old soul'? Or someone rather dull, uninteresting and naïve – a person with a very young soul? When I was a child, my mum would often say to me, 'You've been here before.' So do souls move on again and again? In the end, with my faith, I'll let God be the judge of this and of the role of cryonics. Some priests feel that there is no conflict between cryonics and religion: a priest has even visited the storage facility at CI to bless one of the cryostats. What I do know is that, for me as a person and as a professional, freedom of choice is hugely important, whatever my own views might be.

Although I cannot join my cryonicist colleagues in true spirit, I can certainly assist them by doing my job professionally and exercising this motto of freedom of choice, even though to me the 'patients' have definitely gone and are not just 'pending'. It is my professional duty to assist in the first stage of freezing – the perfusion – as described above, and I will obviously continue to do this as well as I can. Completely professional funeral directors do not choose their clients; instead, they are chosen by the clients and their families to understand and assist in carrying out people's wishes.

Undertakers must not be – and rarely are – the judge of people, although dilemmas can arise if they do not stick to that rule: it is reported that 20 firms refused to carry out the funeral of convicted 'Moors murderer' Myra Hindley.

The funeral director's job is to carefully and professionally dispose of the dead (for everyone's good) and not to make judgement calls. I, like so many others who have read the case and confession of Myra Hindley, cannot help but be affected by this despicable crime, but someone somewhere has to complete her final departure. It might have been better to assist the state and gladly send her on her way at no charge to the taxpayer as a 'duty to mankind', but what you could not do was leave her to rot and continue to affect society. Things have to brought to an end so that we can move on. My thoughts and prayers will be for ever with her victims and their families, but whatever we feel professionally, her departure had to be completed and was done so by a colleague of mine, quietly and with the use of a decoy hearse and evening crematorium service to make sure there was no fuss. If there is a God, and I believe there is, he will be Hindley's judge in the next world. But what would be immoral would be to cryonically suspend her – even giving her that small chance to return would be unacceptable.

With my professional stance at odds with my personal views, my connection with cryonics has often been mis-understood. But you do not have to believe in something in order to complete it: I don't have to jump into a fire to know it is hot! The UK cryonics group on the south coast understands this yet often keeps in touch and lets me know what is going on around the world of cryonics. Last year, the group invited me to a get-together at one of the member's houses. The invitation was for a turkey roast, and on my invitation they had written in jest, 'Welcome, you are invited to a frozen turkey roast with CI members. Will you undertake to come? Arrive early for the defrost.'

See what I mean about their sense of humour?

As well as its work with freezing, the CI has recently moved into keeping, free of charge for its members, DNA samples, which leads me into the very interesting story of Ted Williams. Now if you are English, you will possibly be thinking, who? If you are American though, you will be thinking, what *the* great Ted Williams? Ted Williams, a baseball immortal and now it seems a future immortalist, was a member of the Boston Red Sox and the greatest hitter in the game's history. Ted died in July 2002 and was, after some controversy, reported to have been cryonically suspended at an Alcor facility in Arizona. (Alcor are not part of the CI but are a completely separate group offering suspension at a much higher cost.) This set in motion a wave of publicity reaching further than any of Ted's home runs.

Ted has become the highest-profile immortalist to date. Having taken on the Pirates, the Braves, the Yankees and many other famous baseball teams in life, he was taking on death itself by choosing cryonic suspension. Will Ted be a champion in death as well as life? And did he in fact ever want to be suspended in the first place? The plot thickens. The complicated facts surrounding his suspension have perhaps been best described in a report by David Pascal for *The Immortalist* magazine:

> The bare facts of the case were these: Ted Williams died; subsequently, a new patient, whose name remains confidential, was delivered to the Alcor facility in Arizona; Ted Williams' daughter, Barbara Joyce Ferrell, announced to the press that John Henry Williams, Ted's son, had had his father frozen against his father's

wishes, intending to sell his father's DNA for money; she then announced her intentions to legally acquire her father's remains for burial or cremation, even going so far as to call on President George Bush and Senator John Glenn to intervene.

The accusations flew thick and fast, and negative stories proliferated. Son John Henry Williams was said to have been manipulative, even abusive, in his handling of his father. Associates of Ted Williams crowded the papers and airwaves, contradicting one another as they expressed their certainty that Williams wanted both interments on land and cremation at sea.

Eventually, as facts emerged, the tide turned. Some charges – such as that of selling Williams' DNA – were absurd on the face of it. Why freeze an entire human being for $120,000 to preserve DNA when freezing a few hairs for barely $100 would work just as well? Then Ted Williams' other (and markedly calmer) daughter spoke to the press, confirming that Williams did in fact know what he was doing, and that he wanted to be suspended. John Henry Williams produced paperwork with Ted Williams' signature confirming that wish. It was immediately counter-charged that the signature was faked. (It was not, according to a handwriting analyst.) Then it was claimed that Ted was unfit to decide and/or unaware of what he was signing. But proof of mental debilitation as opposed to claim was not in evidence, and that charge fizzled too. Legal action continues, but uncertainty over whether Ted Williams will remain safely in cryostasis has apparently receded. At the moment, the debate seems to be about which members of the family are most likely to sell the late slugger's bats.

This might seem a little biased because David is a cryonicist, but it is nevertheless intriguing. If it is correct that Ted Williams truly wanted to be suspended, as it seems he now is (for the time being anyway), think how this whole mess could have been avoided had he, while in good health, made a video recording, or a Will, with his solicitor stating his wishes and belief in the science of cryonics, and saying clearly that he had willingly chosen to be treated in the hope that the technology would one day restore him to his old self. Or he could have said completely the opposite and asked for another form of final departure. The salutary lesson here is that however you choose to go, you should be sure to make your wishes well known to all around you, leave no room for error and do all this in sound body and mind – particularly if you are a high-profile personality or your choice of final departure is a controversial one. At least my family know what I want – look out Bermondsey, here I come.

I just hope that immortalists spend more time thinking about the world they live in now and less about the one they may never see. One immortalist has purchased 40 acres just outside Phoenix/Scottsdale in the US. It is a quiet, well-served spot, and if things work out he plans to build a cryonics community there. He would build cabins along the creek, with a hospice and at-home hospice care. Here, like-minded people could live and work together, even sharing their wealth. On the Cryonet website, they are already asking for people with special talents (and already becoming selective) – experts with computer skills, public speakers, media people, publishers, printers, people with different abilities but one common and overwhelming aim – to become an immortalist, perhaps the very first. Such an communal approach, it is thought, will also raise the odds of multiple survival.

This is an interesting proposal but it reminds me a little of what happened in Waco, Texas in 1993, when nearly 80 members of the Branch Davidian cult died having set fire to their own headquarters during a seige by the FBI. The 'Cryo-ville' should of course be the opposite of that as everyone would be wishing to extend their lives and not end them prematurely, but all too many cults seem to tread a narrow line between obsession, sanity and spiritual serenity. Would it not be better instead to join one of the growing number of cryonics support groups – the UK, the US, Canada, Eire, the Netherlands, Belgium and Denmark, for example, all have them?

I truly think that immortalists are very brave. What if this does become a reality and the first people to be defrosted find themselves in unbearable pain or mental agony? What traumas await the cryonics pioneers if their wish ever comes true? Conversely, history has proved pioneers to be essential to the progress of every generation that follows. If cryonics patients are ever successfully revived, there might be many good offshoots. Could those with a terminal illness be suspended and revived when a cure had been found? Could cryonics be used for deep space travel? Will there ever be a cryonics bank storing legs, arms, organs that are frozen ready to be transplanted? Or will other developments in medical science mean that we live so long that there are no parts available to put into a bank? Science could, in time, make either our dreams or our nightmares a reality.

By now, you cannot help but have noticed how passionate I am about people's freedom to choose their own mode of departure, but here is the case of a family who have taken their chosen method of cryonics to quite an extreme in the form of DIY cryonic suspension. Now I may not believe in the eventual success of cryonics, especially of the DIY type, but I will defend the family's right to do this – why should we deny a person the right to wait and see?

Our DIY 'enthusiast' is Remy Martinot, who still shares his home in western France with his mother and father, although these days the latter are residing in a colder part of the house: in the cellar deep below ground, in a home-made cryostat. Monique and Raymond Martinot are, it would seem, the epitome of the word 'pioneer'. Monique was not during life an immortalist; that passion was deeply embodied in her husband, a doctor, who had for some reason always believed that he would die first. He was therefore distraught when she died of cancer before him, in 1984. Monique loved her husband so very much that she agreed to his idea just to please him.

When Monique died in hospital, Raymond applied directly to the mayor, local judge and police, who all agreed to his plan for cryonic suspension. He completed the perfusion himself and then, interestingly, proceeded to arrange a full traditional funeral, including a priest and full Mass, all conducted by a local funeral director. That indicates to me that he was naturally going through the grieving process and had accepted Monique's death, not something that immortalists usually feel, yet it was his long-term hope, like that of true immortalists, to have his wife return one day. Monique, after her standard ceremony of departure, was put into a body bag and placed in the special home-made freezer. It is said that local people, who described Monique as a refined, intellectual who loved music, labelled her 'Sleeping Beauty' because of her stunning dark hair, beautiful pale complexion and unusual fate.

When Raymond died many years later, Remy followed the same procedure and used the same, still operational, freezer to reunite his mum and dad below the house. That old freezer broke down only once, to be repaired by Raymond, still alive at the time. Remy said that his father could not resist a final peep at Monique, who, despite having been dead for many years, was still perfect and very beautiful. Meanwhile, Remy continues to follow his parents' wishes and is completely at one with his duty. He admits grieving for them but just gets on with his life. He does not go and say goodnight to them or open the freezer for a further look. He does not dream of the day that they may return. Instead, he is realistic about the final outcome and is, like any good son, simply respecting his parents' wishes.

Now, none of this was causing anyone any problem. The whole process was respectfully completed (even with a little physical help from the local gendarme, who lifted Raymond into the freezer) with full permission from the authorities. But then a court in Nantes ruled that human remains must be either buried or cremated and that a freezer was not a suitable resting place for them. To me, this seems a bit at odds with the idea that a museum is okay for mummies and a church crypt for bodies, but there you are. Although the freezer is reported to be set at $-80°C$, much higher than the $-196°C$ needed for cryonics, the temperature of non-deterioration, a crypt is in fact likely to be even warmer so decay would be certain. Anyway, the

French authorities said Remy had to defrost Mum and Dad and bury them quickly. Is there any affront to decency or risk to public health here? Of course not, so why can the authorities not leave well alone? To me, this is a breach of human rights.

I think, however, that the real long-term problem will come from Remy's parents in terms of the responsibility that this is placing on their son, ruling his whole life. The wishes of the previous generation can sometimes be too much to live up to. It would make the honourable Remy's life a lot easier if he could send his mum and dad to the CI and let them take the strain. A sad story I think, and I can only hope that there is a peaceful ending.

Perhaps, borrowing some of the sense of humour I have encountered in my cryonicist colleagues, we should leave the last word in the area of cryonics to the actor Woody Allen, himself a reported immortalist: 'I don't want to live on in my films or in any part of my work. I want to live on in my apartment.'

Further reading on Cryonics:

The Immortalist (well presented, interesting and fun)
Cryonics Institute
24355 Sorrentino Court
Clinton Township
MI 48035, USA

The Immortalist
Editorial Office
c/o John Bull
PO Box 372149
Satellite Beach
FL 32973-0149, USA

The Prospect of Immortality, R.C.W. Ettinger, Doubleday/ Immortalist Society (1987)

Man Into Superman, R.C.W. Ettinger, St Martins Press (1972), Immortalist Society (1989)

Engines of Creation, E. Eric Drexler, Doubleday (1986)

Living Longer, Growing Younger, Paul Segall with Carol Kahn, Random House (1989)

The First Immortalist, James Halperin, DelRey Books/ Ballantine (1998)

Forever for All, R. Michael Perry, Universal Publishers (2000)

11

Lights, camera, action!

Back in the late 1970s, an Iranian gentleman once said to me that if the English have one fault (just the one?!), it is that they believe everything they read in the newspapers and are told on television. After a great deal of thought, I concluded that there was some truth in this. I think we do have a tendency to believe what we are told, but I feel that is slowly changing. We are becoming far more critical and a lot more questioning – which must be an improvement. We all know that television has a massive influence on what we think, feel, say and do – it plays such a huge part in our lives these days – and the funeral profession, like any other profession, is far from immune from the power of the media and from being portrayed within it. And our views can be heavily influenced by that. So let's focus the lens on undertaking and take a closer look.

'What would I give at the moment of death for one more moment of life.' How about that for the opening or closing line of a television drama? After all, everybody wants to go to their particular heaven, don't they, but how many of us actually want to die? As a young man (and probably even more so these days), I was an avid television viewer. I remember as a boy watching the series *Route 66*, built around two young guys in a red sports car (how did I know it was red when we only had a black and white television?) who were driving along the eponymous Route 66, the first highway across the US. Each week, these two men would stop at a little town and get involved in some kind of an adventure. Many years later, I can still hum the programme's haunting theme tune, but little did I know then that an undertaker friend would one day be telling me a different sort of tale about Route 66.

A gentleman who had been completely addicted to this old programme and had on many occasions travelled Route 66 in an identical (red) sports car died after a long illness. His dying wish was to be driven one more time by a friend in that beautiful car and to have his cremated remains scattered slowly along the road. The cremation completed, his best friend undertook the final departure, TV style, keeping strictly to the famous road. I think it was a great way to say goodbye to a dear friend, scattering his ashes to the sound of that wonderful theme music; fantastic!

So what other television programmes and films can I think of that will fit here? What effect have they had on the profession or on people's feelings towards their own final departures? And what do I myself think of them? In true gameshow style, here is my own five-plus coffin endorsement ⚰⚰⚰⚰⚰ or five-minus gravestone show of disgust ††††† for them, so go on, will you open the coffin or take the gravestone?

*　　*　　*

In Loving Memory was an early 1980s sitcom starring the wonderful Thora Hird. Filmed in Yorkshire, it told the weekly tales of a local undertaking firm run by the widow of the deceased owner and her nephew, Billy. The stories covered every possible ridiculous angle of the job – a coffin rolling out of the old hearse down the hill and floating out to sea (every undertaker's nightmare), the burial of the wrong body, the hearse breaking down, the pall-bearers having to run along with the coffin when they are late for the service. As there were several series over its long run, it was, in television terms, regarded as successful, but I always found it rather over the top and quite stupid. My thoughts always turned to recently bereaved people who might accidentally have switched on to the programme without knowing; they certainly would not have found it amusing. So, as it was not funny, or sad, but only ridiculous, I am going to give it three gravestones (only the brilliant Thora saving it from a full five minuses).

In Loving Memory: ✝✝✝

The magic five gravestones has, however, been scored by *Fun at the Funeral Parlour*, a new sitcom set in a small undertakers in Wales – definitely not a programme I could bring myself to watch more than once. It is more vulgar, in a modern sense, than *In Loving Memory* and should definitely not be seen by anyone who has recently lost a friend or relative. Starring no one particularly famous, and in my view merely a complete insult to death, this programme deserves the worst of all scores.

Fun at the Funeral Parlour: ✝✝✝✝✝

There is hope though. *Heartbeat*, focusing on the life of a village bobby in the 1960s and full of excellent 60s music, also features the local undertaker, Mr Scripps, and is a very good programme, well worth a mention. Not at all insulting to the funeral business, it is very accurate in portraying the times and very clearly shows how a small-town undertaker could barely scratch a living from his trade, turning as well to a second profession – carpentry, building and so on – to make ends meet. Our Mr Scripps also runs a garage, selling petrol and effecting vehicle repairs. The hearse is used for everything – running around, delivering Christmas trees, even the occasional taxi ride. Allowing for a bit of media exaggeration to keep viewers happy, I will give this two coffins. Funny, interesting and full of well-known faces, its several series attest to its popularity.

Heartbeat: ▮▮

The research behind the wonderful black drama *The Sins*, brilliantly written by William Ivory, has been even more thorough. I would even go so far as to say that it is incredible. William Ivory must have had a connection with the world of funerals, so many remarkable poignant moments of grief being dealt with throughout the series.

Starring Pete Postlethwaite, Geraldine James and Frank Finlay among others, *The Sins* is the story of Len Green (Pete Postlethwaite), a man in crisis. After four and a half years in prison, and having more than provided for his family during a life of crime, he decides to go straight and earn an honest living. But just how will his wife Gloria and his daughters, Faith, Hope, Chastity, Charity and Dolores, adjust to their new-found, but much less influential, status? And will it really be so easy for Len to resist the temptations offered by his criminal past, particularly when his old cohorts are so reluctant to let him go? His only salvation is his Uncle Irwin (Frank Finlay), who offers him a job in his long-established undertaking business as a means to the end of an honest living. As Len confronts each sin and client, Irwin remains confident that he will learn one thing above all else: that the greatest virtue of all in life – and death – is love.

Although we have to remember that the writer's aim was to investigate the moral aspects of sin rather than issues from the world of death and the undertaker, many of Uncle Irwin's philosophies seem to come straight from my own 'Rules for a Life in Death' and 'Philosophies of Death':

- It's already bad enough – don't make it any worse.
- One funeral at a time – don't ever take the goodness from the job.
- The answer is yes – now ask the question.
- If you have compassion and love in your heart, your brain will always follow.
- Glass we see clearly through on all but two occasions in our lives – our birth and our death. At birth, we need a midwife to help us into this world and see clearly into the future. At death, the undertaker becomes the midwife who helps you leave this life clearly. Perhaps there is a third when we fall in love?
- Like me, Uncle Irwin finds the saddest part of his job dressing people who have died in their new shoes. New shoes put on a dead person will never go anywhere. I find that very sad and a stark reminder of my own mortality, which keeps my feet firmly on the ground.
- Bereavement is the dreadful burden that death lays

upon us. I say again, the only way forward is to get up each day, put one foot in front of the other and just see what the day will bring. There is no magic solution – patience, care and, as always, hope are needed, but most important are time and love.

- This world will keep on spinning with its own agenda no matter what I do, think, feel or believe. In the big picture, we are all very much surplus to requirements, yet the sum of all our contributions can make an amazing difference.

- Life is very fragile, and we totter daily on the brink of life and death. If there comes a time in our lives when we honestly recognise that, each day thereafter is a little more precious to us.

- The most sacred word of all when facing ourselves, our friends, our life and, eventually and most importantly, our death is 'atonement'. For me, atonement is not the end of the world but true reality that can be summed up in the simple translation 'At – One – Ment'. In the Church, the act of atonement occurs in the moment when we see clearly and come to understand, when we are 'contrite', truly sorry in ourselves. Only when we are at one with our vulnerability, and see our weakness and our inner self, can we be capable of *forgiveness* and therefore truly know ourselves, allowing us to see through the glass of life and death without a reflection of the past. At that one moment, we can answer the truth only by speaking with our hearts. We will be able to come to terms with our losses by understanding ourselves and the inner anger that haunts us. We have to search for this forgiveness to release the poison that will otherwise cripple us in the rest of our life's journey.

*   *   *

In all my life, I have never linked myself so strongly with any person, fictional or real, as I have with Frank Finlay's Uncle Irwin. My life in Bermondsey as a funeral director is a gift, but one that can weigh heavily on me, my family and my friends. I am often invited to deliver the eulogy for some of the families I serve, and then, after the funeral, I am always invited back to the wake. But I am rarely invited to other parties, well as I know people in Bermondsey, not because I am a misery (well, I hope not, although I must confess that I am not much of a party animal), but because I cross their minds only at times of loss. Nobody wants to be reminded of death when experiencing wonderful moments of joy – weddings, birthdays, christenings. I hope they do not like me any less because of my profession, but there is a time and a place for everything and everyone.

My sons seem to have managed that area of their lives better than I have: Jonathan has an excellent social life with his fiancée and her family, and Simon has achieved a very good balance between work and play. They will one day run the business; I hope they will not let it rule them as it does me. They have the right to put themselves – and their families – first, without guilt. Many people forget that an undertaker has a life outside his or her profession, and that it is important to have other interests and a release from the stresses of the job. Uncle Irwin, like me, suffers from others' assumptions and expectations, but he too feels he has a purpose outside funeral directing: despite all his correctness, propriety and respectability, he enjoys rock music and happily plays it when he is making coffins or embalming in the evenings.

Like all of us, Uncle Irwin needs emotional comfort; this

he has sought and quietly found. Uncle Irwin has tragically lost a son (I pray this never happens to me), and the only mention of a wife is to say that she has died. However, unbeknown to anyone, Uncle Irwin has a girlfriend to comfort him. Without people close to you, it is hard to find your way, and loneliness, as Uncle Irwin constantly finds, can be a dreadful adversary. I find it all too easy to understand how running an emotional business such as undertaking is very isolating no matter how many people are around you. Like me, Uncle Irwin knows the burden of responsibility that being the guardian of such a business can bring, and both of us accept our responsibilities. As I look around me at all the ledgers carrying the family names of people in the parish and more recently around the world, I realise that I am the custodian of their memories, the keeper of the key of their past. I hope I continue to do this and that computers do not take over this task, as they have so many others.

So who counsels the counsellor? How do funeral directors handle their own grief? A tricky question. Funeral directors share the same right to grieve, and if our guard is down, we are more vulnerable. I have known many funeral directors who have taken their own lives or become alcoholics. Some have businesses that have failed; others have found personal bereavement too much to handle while dealing with the burden of grief of those they serve. Some have not been able to cope with the historical responsibility of the position they hold. No one can be blamed for such actions; to know the truth, we must first walk for a while in the other person's shoes, and that can rarely be achieved.

In *The Sins*, Uncle Irwin has, some might say, apparently silly or disrespectful ways of dealing with some moments of his grief, knowing that his son, who died aged 17, had always been too young to reap the benefit of his father's well-earned wisdom. Uncle Irwin consoles himself by visiting his son's grave after hours to talk to him and reinforce – and then release – his anger that his son never listened to the few words of advice that might have extended his life. Uncle Irwin leaps over the gravestones to show his son that he is not past it, reiterates the value of wisdom and, more importantly, looks for atonement from his son for perhaps not using the wisdom of an old man to listen to a young one. 'Forgiveness' has to come from all sides to be effective.

But perhaps my greatest affiliation with Uncle Irwin will be in death. In the last show, he dies in the arms of probably the only person in the world who perhaps loved him for himself and knew him for who he truly was – his girlfriend, a brothel madam (not that I'm suggesting that for my end!). His death completely changes Len. Uncle Irwin's parting gift is to leave Len the business and, more importantly, the historical responsibility and the fortitude to fulfil it. Len immediately recognises this and sees all that Uncle Irwin has been trying to teach him. When Len declares, 'I am a funeral director like my Uncle Irwin', my first thought was, 'Fantastic; that touched me deeply', my second, 'You've done it now, mate.' For the rest of his life, Len is sincere, the guardian of so many memories, the greatest perhaps those of Uncle Irwin, God bless him. Even though Uncle Irwin is a fictional character, I am sure that there are still a few Uncle Irwins around in real life.

Uncle Irwin's funeral was, for me, perfect. When he was alive, he never knew the true effect of the work he was doing locally (indeed, who would?). If he could have seen his own funeral, I am sure his whole life would, for the first time, have made complete sense, banishing all those moments of doubt that we all have about our own existence. Endless flowers, a motorboat, a horse-drawn hearse, a final burial with his beloved son. It was as if the whole of North London came out to pay their respects to this humble but wonderful man whose true appreciation was there clear to see in the faces and numbers of mourners present. 'He had made a difference'; who could ask for more? Certainly not me. I would like to be half as good a man as Frank Finlay's portrayal and William Ivory's description of someone he truly understands.

Definitely five coffins – the best.

The Sins: ♟♟♟♟♟

Another absolute winner is *Six Feet Under*, written and produced by the amazing Alan Ball of *American Beauty* movie fame. This programme is set to run and run, maybe even to gain cult status. So who are the key characters in this wonderfully black look at the world of undertaking?

The dead dad, Nathaniel Fisher (Richard Jenkins), meets his Maker in a crash with a bus while driving his new hearse. When he was alive, he liked secretly smoking pot and wearing Bermuda shorts as he worked; after death, he continues to appear in his family's minds. Nathaniel's neurotic wife Ruth (Frances Conroy) turns when her husband dies: after a life full of death, she decides she is sick of dead people.

Slacker son Nate, played by Peter Kraus, is a college drop-out who has never held down a proper job or relationship. When his father dies, he is left 50 per cent of the business, forcing him to face up to the responsibility. His gay brother

David (Michael Hall), whose sexuality is a secret, joined the family firm at 20. He resents his elder brother's freedom: while Nate got to enjoy college parties, David ended up draining corpses. He really wants to go to law school, or does he? Their sister Claire (Lauren Ambrose) is stoned when she hears that her dad has died. At school, she is deemed a freak because she drives a bright green hearse.

Completing the line up are Nate's mixed-up girlfriend Brenda Chenowith (Rachel Griffiths) and make-up man and junior Frederico Diaz (Freddy Rodriguez). Brenda was declared a genius at six and put in the care of psychiatrists who wrote a book about her. Frederico is a young dad, one of the best 'restorative artists' for corpses, is proud of his work.

In an article I was asked to write for the *Sun* newspaper in 2002, reviewing the first four episodes of the series, I wrote: 'In the opening minutes of the first episode there is a violent death, sex, drugs and swearing. It might make you think it's just another American attempt to shock us – but as you keep watching you realise that this is a remarkable series.' For all its over-the-top characters and underpinning, and the fact that some of its scenes are designed to shock, the programme is very special and based on very good research. It certainly mirrors episodes from my own life:

There's a brilliant flashback when the dad is embalming someone and his sons Nate and David come in. He tells them not to be scared and to touch the body if they want.

The same thing happened when I was washing and looking after bodies. My young sons Simon, who is

26 now, and his brother Jonathan, who is 23, would come in. I didn't ever close any doors. I let my kids understand what was going on, that death is a part of life and facing it is the big mystery and the final hurdle to true undertaking

The embalmers talk to the bodies too, which I always do, not because I'm mad but because you have to remember that you are dealing with a person . . .

In the first episode of *Six Feet Under*, one of the sons, David, attempts to restore his father to how he looked when he was alive but he finds it very difficult. I can understand that. My mother died when I was 17 and I was totally numbed by it. So was my father, himself an undertaker in Bermondsey and Rotherhithe . . .

One of the families in the show gets really angry at his father's funeral organised by the Fishers. I've seen people lose it at funerals and start fights. It is so unhealthy to contain grief.

The opening sequence of each episode is, to me, truly descriptive of the narrow margin between life and death, the hanging on to and letting go of life. First comes a very clever catchy tune backed up by poignant opening scenes: an empty, clear blue sky broken by a black bird winging its way across to announce the impending doom, followed by two hands (male and female) grasping each other, clinging onto life, which break to show separation. Hands being washed in sterile preparation for dealing with the dead. The camera focuses on the base of the trolley holding the deceased and pans up to a shot of the feet, the dreaded toe tag marking the arrival of the dead. Back to clear sky, the blue and white changing to a shiny green, before the shot switches to a turning wheel on the trolley. The trolley is moving along a corridor, leaving a shadow of a person in the light and heading towards a new light (like leaving one world for another).

The shot that follows, which includes an operating embalming technician, is taken from one side of a canopic embalming jar full of clear liquid, the fluid slowly but subtly being sucked from the jar into the deceased. Now we see the side of a man's head, a man in his early 30s maybe, the eye being shown as the embalmer cleans it (the preparing of the dead for the final departure). The next shot shows the hands of the deceased, but they have become a woman's hands, maybe to show that death is not selective. Then we see a bouquet of flowers bursting into life and dying in fast-frame – the blossoming of life and its brevity, death speeding towards it.

The following section is shot from inside the hearse, a hand lifting the casket handle and beginning to pull the coffin from the hearse for its final few yards journey, leaving the empty vehicle with its door open. We are then directed to two photographs and back to the black bird, claws over a branch and hovering like the Sword of Damacles. The casket crosses the frame, carried by the appointed pall-bearers. We now see the cemetery, with its gravestones, for the first time before our view switches to the waiting black bird and then the blue skies, a field, a single tree, as the black bird flies from the scene for the last time. All that is left is the tree, which is then bathed in a bright light synonymous with death. Throughout the opening sequences, the credits appear on embalming jars, on gravestones, on caskets, on a hearse – fascinating.

The whole opening concept concerns the fragility of life and the ever-ready battery of death. The pilot programme opens when David Fisher has said how restful a man's wife looks in her casket, to be met with the mourner's words 'If there is any justice in the universe, she's shovelling shit in hell' (pardon the language). Believe me, that sort of incident too is not far from the truth. My dad once showed a lady into the chapel to see her late husband in his coffin. 'He looks very peaceful', Dad said. Came the reply, 'The old bastard should have died years ago, sod him.'

But back to fiction. Pa Fisher's death has left the whole family confused, numb, angry, full of denial and depressed – as I have said before, even funeral directors and their families are not exempt from the stages of grief. What unfolds is intriguing to say the least and, despite being rather over the top, not a little frightening as I see the similarities with my own life brought to the forefront of my mind. Living in and above the funeral home, growing up and being introduced to the final departures of the families who pass through the home, becoming a young funeral director, the 24-hour pressure that responsibility brings. Unlike the Fishers, I undertook the whole journey without the support of brothers or sisters, but, from the beginning of the series, the boys are united, in conflict, under pressure, short of money and pursued for purchase by a massive American funeral company that seems to have obtaining the little Fisher family firm as its sole purpose in life – which I did not find very realistic.

In one episode, the pressure overcomes the Fishers and they agree to sell. After signing a Head of Agreement and collecting a cheque for the deposit, David, who has been running the business with his dad and taking on the main day-to-day responsibility, describes to his partner his feelings, moments, and again hours, after the signing. I have always harboured, and longed to temporarily experience, such feelings! David says that he walked from the room after the signing feeling absolutely wonderful, as if the worries of the world had been lifted from his shoulders. The responsibility of the grief and sacred care of the dead was no longer his. He did not have to open the funeral home tomorrow or employ anyone. No bills to pay, no cleaning, no time to balance, no one dead to prepare, no more 'juicing' (as they often call embalming in the US) – someone else would be doing all those things. For the first time ever in his life, he was truly *free*. Boy, would I love to know just how that feels.

But a few hours later, David's real feelings rear up to haunt him, as I know they would me. He feels he has no purpose anymore, just emptiness. He feels lonely, unhappy, guilty, sad. He has begun to understand his value and how important the funeral home, his father's legacy and his calling are to his very existence. He cannot let it go. So David immediately exercises the seven-day cooling-off period, happily tears up the cheque and, with a full appreciation of the true value of his work and life, opens the funeral home with a new step in his stride. What must have shocked him even more is that his brother feels the same and happily tears up his cheque too.

The last show in the present series ends with Nate facing a struggle for life and death. He is undergoing neurological surgery, from which he could wake up fine or wake up a vegetable – or not wake up at all. We are treated to a view from inside Nate's mind while he is under the anaesthetic. He is standing on the side of a never-ending road when a bus stops and the door opens. Could it be the bus that killed his dad? There is no driver, no one else even on the bus. Nate stands at the door as a white light engulfs the screen. We do not know whether Nate gets on the bus (which of course represents death itself) or comes back for a further series. Someone once said that if you throw the letters of the word FUNERAL up in the air, they could come down as REAL FUN (or RUN LEAF or RAN FUEL or NAFLERU or any other jumble), and 'real fun' is probably how Nate saw his life before his father's death. Sadly, however, that's not how it is when you are on the receiving end of death or bereavement.

Now, you are probably thinking that this is only a television show and not reality. But these people become part of your home for an hour every week, and the story line is based so closely on the truth and probably also on actual stories experienced by real-life people, that it certainly grabs hold of you for a while, which seems to have come over in how I have described it. I truly believe that *Six Feet Under* has had an amazing influence on society and the funeral profession, which seems to have received it with mixed emotions. As I wrote in my *Sun* review: 'Overall, I'm not sure we Brits are ready for such a black comedy about the funeral business. But we have to face up to death and this programme will help people deal with bereavement.' So, as far as I'm concerned, five coffins for this one. Definitely a cult programme not to be missed.

Six Feet Under: ⚰⚰⚰⚰⚰

In the US, a more way-out style in television entertainment seems to be much more acceptable than it is in the UK, in the same way that advertising the funeral profession is more acceptable there. So where might we go next – *Undertakers in Space?* Well, as I finish writing this chapter, Albin's is three months into making its own documentary, *Don't Drop the Coffin!*, which is being filmed by Ginger TV, a branch of Scottish Television, for the ITV network. The 30-minute episodes are to be shown weekly over a six-week period. For me, this documentary will be the definitive programme about this firm and indeed the funeral industry. It certainly opens us up to scrutiny so agreeing to its production reflects my huge confidence in those who work at Albin's. I sincerely hope that it will break down some of the stigmas and taboos surrounding death and positively influence the public's perception of the funeral business and how dying is handled. Time of course will tell. At the very least, for good or bad, it will be a recorded history of three generations of the firm. Whether it is loved or hated, I am glad that I have had the courage to undertake it. All credit must also go to my sons and all the staff for their dedication and support throughout. He who dares wins – I hope!

12
The final frontier

'The needs of the many outweigh the needs of the few . . . or the one.' Mr Spock's last words when he sacrificed his own life to save those of his crewmates in the Star Trek movie *The Wrath of Khan*. People were killed every week in the television programmes – and even more of them in the movie series – but what is really strange is that you never see a funeral director. There are scientific teams, security teams, research teams, engineers, but who sends the dead on their final departure? Why is there no black mourning uniform? No undertaking squad? As I watched Spock being shot from the starboard bow torpedo tube in his hermetically sealed, shiny black coffin, I could not help wondering whether we would ever be doing such a thing with the dead. No, of course not, I remember concluding at the time, but how wrong I was. A final departure in space is now indeed a reality. Our next hearse is unlikely to be the 'Albin's Enterprise', but who knows what will happen a hundred years from now?

My visions of *Undertakers in Space* took a step nearer reality in June 1999 when I undertook the funeral of Alan Mihara, a successful Japanese businessman who had died in his home in Bermondsey aged just 43 years. His charming wife Naomi came to us to arrange what she described as a beautiful farewell, and I have to agree that it truly *was* beautiful: a traditional English horsedrawn funeral, unusual and lovely flowers and a carefully planned family service and reception.

Naomi Mihara was the epitome of kindness and thoughtfulness for others. I am sure that is how she coped with the dreadful pain she was inwardly feeling. For her, there was still her lovely daughter, her family, the business and her work to be considered, as well as the funeral itself. Although we did not know it at the outset, there were still three stages of saying goodbye to go through, the initial one being a first for us too. Some of Mr Mihara's ashes were to be floated into the sea from his favourite spot just off the coast of Swanage on a bright August morning at dawn. The Albin's staff were kindly invited to stay in a local hotel the night before and enjoy an evening meal with Naomi, which they did. At dawn, friends and family gathered at the dock, where a boat was waiting. At this point, Naomi and her family spoke from the heart about Alan. Everyone then placed a personal message into a metal container, which was then burnt, the ashes being mixed with Alan's.

Together, everyone present boarded the boat and gently moved off to the outskirts of the coast. At the appropriate moment of calm, accompanied by the sunrise, lovely words and personal family participation, the ashes, in an open basket smothered with fresh sunflowers, were lowered by Greg and Jamie (from Albin's) and the family into the water. As the boat drew slowly away, the ashes floated away, leaving a long line of sunflowers stretching into the distance. The family then returned to a beachfront restaurant, just by the spot where the basket had been floated into the sea, where Alan and Naomi had often enjoyed a meal. Here, all enjoyed a champagne breakfast and a wonderful chance to reminisce. Could any final departure be more perfect?

Two small containers of ashes had, however, by instruction, been retained. Naomi had purchased, in perpetuity for her family, a columbarium in our sanctuary within the cremation cemetery. Here, she will, with a small ceremony, deposit a portion of those remaining ashes and, in accordance with tradition, Alan's first cut of hair – a small teenage ponytail. One last addition to this incredible and loving tradition is Alan's umbilical cord, cut at birth and kept sacredly by his parents throughout his mere 43 years of life. But what of the remaining tube of ashes? Later this year, they will be shot into space, 'the final frontier', something I never thought I would see.

The company that undertakes this service is Celestis Commemorative Space Flights, for which we are now the UK agents. With the service, clients receive

- the launch of a symbolic portion of the cremated remains into space;
- a flight capsule imprinted with a personal message;
- an invitation to the launch;
- a personalised video of the launch event and memorial ceremony;
- a dedicated virtual memorial to the deceased on the Celestis website;

- a contribution to the Celestis Foundation;
- performance assurance.

Various options are available. In the Earthview Service I, one gram of the cremated remains is sent into earth's orbit. With the Earthview Service II (Naomi's personal choice), a seven-gram sample is used instead. The Celestis Lunar Service places the cremated remains into lunar orbit or on to the lunar surface, whereas the Voyager Service launches the cremated remains into deep space on an infinite journey among the stars. The Ad Astra Service, available to all clients regardless of their choice of final disposition, transmits a high-powered digital memorial (including a photograph and a biography) to the stars and includes a Star Registry certificate commemorating the naming of a star in memory of you or your loved one. Isn't it amazing to think that we could be whizzing through space for all eternity? As Buzz Lightyear says in the film *Toy Story* – 'To infinity and beyond!'

But I am not sure that space can be viewed as the only 'final frontier' for our last send-off. How about the depths of the ocean? It is still possible to be buried at sea, although there are defined requirements for the sort of coffin you can have and the area you can be buried on. Alternatively, a company called Eternal Reefs promises an eternity below the sea that will benefit the environment while offering another option of final resting place. It seems that Eternal Reefs can take cremated remains and integrate them into what they describe as natural-looking and aesthetically pleasing artificial reef structures called reef balls. These are placed under the sea, where they help to generate new aquatic life and revive an endangered ecosystem, making us less environmentally destructive than we ever were in life. There are, apparently, over 100,000 state-of-the-art reef balls in place around the globe.

The finished product looks more like one of those pots full of holes that you turn upside down so that things can grow through it, but once positioned in the sea, plant life soon grows over the reef ball, fish breed inside it and it becomes part of the coral area. The area is then registered as a 'memorial reef'. A nice touch is that you can break the solitude of the sea by visiting the area, or even diving down to the reef, to spend a few quiet moments with your loved one. Many people will find this a very attractive idea, but I do not think it is really for me. If I ended up in a reef ball, it would have to go into the Thames for me to feel at home, and I doubt it would do much for the price of riverfront property at low tide, even if it would provide a perfect home for the eels.

Is there any kind of final departure that you cannot have? One 'gem' of an idea with a certain charm to it is the making of diamonds from the bone ash of cremated remains, both diamonds and the human body being carbon based. They say that 'Diamonds are for ever', don't they? – well, now it could be true of you too. Synthetic diamonds have been manufactured from carbon since the mid-1950s, originally by General Electric Co., who produced diamonds for industrial use, so the overall idea is nothing new.

These diamonds are called 'life gems', and it is said that they are completely impossible to distinguish from other synthetic diamonds. So how is the transformation made? First, the cremated remains are purified in a vacuum induction furnace at 3000°Celsius (about 5400°Fahrenheit). The product is then placed in a press under intense pressure and heat, recreating the forces that make a natural diamond. The whole process takes about four months. The diamonds are, according to Greg Herro, the head of Life Gem Memorials of Chicago, which makes them, of the same quality as those you might find at Tiffany's jewellers.

For a cost of $4000 at today's rates, Life Gem Memorials can make a small thimbleful of carbon into a 0.25 carat diamond, a full carat costing around $22,000. If you have the money, it seems a very loving idea. In Bermondsey, I have met plenty of what we call 'diamond geezers' but to date no geezer who has actually become a diamond.

So now, on our journey, we have come full circle back to Bermondsey. The final departures we have encountered – some interesting, some sad, others bizarre, one or two very funny – all have in common the fact that they *are* final (although I know the cryonicists would want to argue that one). The funerals I have been involved with in South London are certainly those I know and love best, so it seems fitting to remember some of the special ones. And as the companies we have encountered so far in this chapter are all American, let's start with the first Americans I ever met.

In my youth, my dad undertook a funeral for an American family who had lost their mother to a massive heart attack during a world tour stopover in London; we had been recommended to the family by Nuffield House, the private wing of Guy's Hospital. After much deliberation, the family decided to have their mother cremated, aiming to collect her ashes on their return to the UK, at which point they would escort her to New York on the liner the *Queen Mary*. It had always been their mother's ambition to cruise the Atlantic on the *Queen Mary*, and in some small way the family wanted to fulfil her wishes. The cremation was arranged at our local crematorium, and Dad introduced me to the family, who had taken a shine to the old Dickensian shop of Albin's – and to my Dad too.

In those days, all our cremation coffins were covered in a kind of mauve material (horrible material, I always thought, but that was what all the funeral directors used). Dad, however, had managed to obtain one roll of grey material, which had enough on it for one more coffin. The American family loved it and wanted their mother's coffin covered in it, with silver fittings. So far, so good. The funeral was a simple cremation with just the family present, and Dad collected the ashes to hold on to until the family's return. But there was one problem: the family wanted the urn containing the ashes to be covered in the same grey material that had been used for the coffin. They were intending to keep the urn in their New York apartment, and matching the grey cloth of the coffin would be a meaningful and symbolic gesture. They hoped that my dad would do his best to match the material that had been on the now fully used roll.

Typical of my Dad, he did everything to get another roll from our supplier, but it was hopeless. We could not find even a small piece to cover the urn. But then Mum observed that the grey material that had been used for the coffin was very similar to a pair of grey trousers my Dad had just purchased. Now Dad loved those trousers. A perfect fit; lovely grey flannels, as my mum had observed when they had chosen them. Back they went to the shop – Grahams Menswear in the Jamaica Road – but, alas, they had finished with that line of grey trouser. There was only one thing left to do. Out came the scissors, and Mum cut up the trousers before Dad could change his mind. When the family returned to the UK, they were duly presented with the urn and ashes at the Grosvenor Hotel on a Sunday afternoon by both Mum and Dad. The family loved it and were very grateful for all that my parents had done. So somewhere in New York, probably to this very day, lies an urn full of ashes covered with the left leg of my Dad's irreplaceable, new grey flannel trousers.

Another colourful incident occurred after the typical cockney funeral of a local docker. The priest, who had delivered wonderfully chosen words of comfort during the service, was warmly embraced afterwards by the family, who insisted he return with them to the wake. This was in itself fine, but the priest was unable to keep up with the drinking. He eventually left the house in the early hours as drunk as could be, walked along the road for a few yards and collapsed through a shop window, only to end up in hospital. Having severed an artery, he was only an inch from hearing his own eulogy delivered. Needless to say, his bishop moved him onto a quieter parish in the country. I often think of him – a smashing man (in more ways than one!).

My good friend Fred Collins, the wonderful local character who, with his own car, worked with me for many years, was recently subject to his own near miss. We were at Forest Hill Cemetery, a very wet cemetery as the ground is mostly clay. The grave-diggers had been working all morning trying to keep the water out of the grave they were working on (not an easy profession, grave-digging) but were fighting a losing battle. In the end, they were forced to remove the top grave supports in order to allow the coffin to pass gently down. I asked the family to stand back from the grave for their own safety, at least until the coffin had

216

been safely lowered, and we managed to get the coffin to the side of the grave that was best supported.

There were, as required, four people to lower the coffin, and I was to support and guide the head of the coffin as it moved across the grave prior to lowering. I stepped back so that Fred could get across to his position, but, as he moved across me on the edge of the grave, it started to collapse, and poor Fred began to be sucked down. Panic set in. Instinctively and without a second thought, I grabbed Fred; he grabbed me back in a last desperate effort not to be buried alive. To those watching, this must have looked very funny as Fred struggled to stay above ground, aimlessly treading water and getting nowhere, but it really was a serious and dangerous moment. Fred is a tall, heavily built man, and it took all my strength to hang on to him, but nothing could have made me let go – I think the world of old Fred.

Well, by now we were up to our knees in mud and water. With all our grave-walking, we must have looked as if we were on one of those fairground attractions with the moving floors that go up and down so all you can see from a distance is people's heads bobbing up and down on the spot. With one huge effort, I managed to yank a very dirty and shocked Fred from the grave. By now, the other lads had joined in too, and after about 10 seconds, which seemed more like 10 minutes, we were back from the edge. It is easy to laugh about it now, but the thought of being buried alive in a 10-foot grave was definitely not amusing at the time. I think Fred saw the thousand funerals he has been part of flash before his eyes. Needless to say, he has been taking things a lot easier since.

Speed was definitely of the essence for Fred, but it is not

always quite so beneficial. Indeed, the velocity of a new cremation charger at a London Crematorium is enough to knock you completely for six. From our Hitchcock's branch in East London, we were conducting a funeral for a large Hindu family. They had used us many times before and knew well the procedure at crematoriums – or so we all thought.

In the Hindu faith, it is traditional for the immediate family to ignite the flame and help to move the coffin into position in the cremator. Modern cremators such as this one at this London Crematorium are extremely efficient and can be very dangerous. For the cremation to be successfully completed, the coffin must be moved quickly, yet safely, into the middle. To assist with this, technicians have designed the cremation charger, a kind of conveyor belt with steel hooks on the rollers that ejects the coffin at speed into the centre of the cremator as required.

Neither Lee, who was conducting the funeral, nor the six family members involved had ever witnessed this machine in action before. Lee took the family into the cremation area. Peter, the cremation operator, a very experienced and kind gentleman, asked Lee to assemble the family in position behind the coffin and told them not to be alarmed by the noise of the charger. All was now set: the family were in position, Peter was wearing his goggles and ready to go, and Lee was confident that all would be fine, having witnessed many such cremations (although not with the charger) before. Peter pressed the button and the cremator door opened to expose the raging furnace inside, that alone enough to upset any bereaved family member. Peter now pressed the charger button, and, with a tremendous thud, the coffin was sent on its way. With a bang, it entered the oven, which was at a slightly different level, the rollers still rumbling. Then the oven door slammed shut for the cremation to begin.

Now, this all happened in seconds. The procedure is very safe but, as Peter warned, very noisy, and by Lee's own admission, it terrified even him. He turned round to the family only to find that three had fainted and the other three were on the floor trying to bring them round while panicking and in a state of shock themselves. Can you imagine the scene? Peter grabbed a glass of water, and one of the mourners began to sprinkle it on the three relatives in their dead faint: 'Wake up, oh my goodness', he cried. Lee opened the door and correctly suggested that they all give them some air as he proceeded to make them more comfortable. Within a few moments, the three individuals had recovered, only to realise what they had just witnessed. That charger is a marvellous piece of machinery, which definitely helps with the safety procedure, but could truly give you a heart attack, especially when you are already grieving, stressed and under pressure. Not to be recommended.

A rather more comforting sound than that of the charger is the music of the bagpipes. It is not uncommon these days for bereaved families, especially those who are of Scottish or Irish descent, to request a piper. The piper normally meets the mourners at the gates of the cemetery or crematorium, playing them in and out of the chapel and again piping when the family are at the graveside or looking at the flowers at the crematorium. Unfortunately, things do not always go smoothly, and indeed two very funny moments concerning the pipes come to mind here.

The first occurred during a service at our local church in

Dockhead. The piper decided to enter the church at the point at which the Communion was being celebrated and play while the family were going up to receive Communion. Bear in mind that no one expected him to do this and that the acoustics in this particular church were very powerful. Well, the noise was deafening. I quickly moved towards him, signalling for him to stop. But he panicked and lost what I believe they call the chanter off the bottom of the bag. It sounded just like a strangled cat as he struggled to hold the bag and bring the pipes under control – very funny in retrospect but *very* embarrassing at the time.

The second mishap brought a smile to the faces of the mourners clustered around one graveside service and, to this day, still makes me chuckle whenever I think of it. It was a misty afternoon at a London Victorian cemetery. As the priest gave the blessing around the grave, the piper, exactly on cue, piped up with *Flowers of the Forest* and began to move off into the misty distance. Tears were falling at this very beautiful moment, the close of the funeral. Then, without warning, the piper just disappeared. 'He's gone', was the cry. 'No he's not, he's back again!' – and he popped back up, hat crooked but still piping, determined that the show would go on. The poor piper had fallen down a part-dug grave, left uncovered when the grave-digger popped off to have his lunch. It was only about four feet deep, but that was enough to bury our little piper. The tears of sadness soon became tears of laughter. It was another one of those precious moments that show people that life is all around them and goes on. The family said it was Mum's way of saying goodbye and showing that she understood – 'Bye, all's well.' I am not sure though that the piper found it quite as comforting.

However, the complications I encounter are sometimes caused not by chance but by those involved, even by those who have died. The machinations of their lives can be highlighted rather than concluded by death. We received one telephone call from a very distressed lady who had just lost her partner after a sudden heart attack. We were her first call, and she wanted to be sure she would get the best final departure possible. A lovely casket, a service in a beautiful old private church, plenty of mourners, limousines, flowers: you name it, this kind, caring lady wanted it. But, in the final stages of planning, all this was brought to an abrupt end when she rang to cancel the funeral and rearrange it as a non-attended, direct disposal funeral. What had changed the good lady's mind was that she had discovered that her partner had, for quite some time, been living a double life with another woman. The two ladies knew nothing of each other, but were in agreement now that neither wanted to have anything to do with him in death. I hope that they do not regret their actions when their anger subsides and the reality becomes evident.

If the gentleman concerned had pre-arranged his own funeral, he might have got the final departure he wanted and not the one he was given. It is definitely a good idea to have your say while you can, to pre-plan it and work all the details out. Don't think that your wishes are silly or will not be understood. What matters is you: it is your death after all.

One of the happiest pre-arranged funerals I have witnessed took place last year. The lady who had died was in her 80s and, in her time on earth, had been a lover of life in every way. To the very end, she was jovial, energetic and youthful, as reflected in her funeral. On her very elegant coffin was placed a pair of dancing shoes. All the family came out to the hearse as it pulled up at the house and touched the coffin to say hello to this incredible lady. They were not dressed in black but instead wore lively party clothes for this was to be a true celebration of her life. The service was full of music and amusing personal tributes, and all the flowers were white. After the service, everyone retired to a local pub for lunch and a toast of vintage champagne to celebrate a splendid life. After the toast, every last champagne flute was smashed into a bin full of bricks as a parting gesture. This truly confirms my belief that final departures can be, and should be, wonderful moments to be cherished. And what of my own? Well, we'll all have to wait and see! Perhaps I'll write another book and let you know.

Many people ask why am I an undertaker (aside from my natural heritage of course). It is because, in the abundance of this life, for all its anguish, its pain and its wrongs, *it is still life*. I look at the shoes of dead people, not the brand new ones that people buy specially in their sadness and may rarely be used again; the shoes *I* look at have been walked in, filled with the energy of this world and of life itself. For all life's ills, for every dreadful moment, there are thimblefuls of joy and contentment that outweigh everything else. The dead never leave us. They are a force always with us until our dying breath brings us final peace.

And what of my purpose as an undertaker? I want the bereaved to look into my eyes, acknowledging all I have seen and done, and see *no fear*, only strength, and from that strength gain hope. Through this, they may see how priceless and precious is the time that we have been given; they may then start living again and put death where it belongs – at the end of life.

Appendix:

Possible methods of final departure

Burial
Earth burial
Brick grave burial
Vault burials
Crypt burials
Mausoleum burial
Catacombs
Burial at sea
Bone burial
Above-ground burial
Sealed-glass viewing chamber
Woodland burials
Donation of remains
for medical science
Ashes/bones in breast implants

Cremation
Scattering of ashes unlimited
Burial of ashes
Depositing ashes into a coral reef
Ashes held in urns
Shooting ashes into space
Ashes put into an egg-timer
Ashes mingled into a painting
Ashes blown into glass
Ash mausoleum
Columbarium/ashebarium
Ashes made into diamonds
Ashes scattered into the sea

A few of my favourites are the following:

- Cryonic Suspension: Ted Williams, an American baseball hero and big hitter in life, but still to record a score in suspension.
- Freeze-Drying: A cow – the first client to this service.
- Unique Burial: A man embalmed and placed in a glass case in London who is still brought out for Governors' meetings.
- Cremation: Canaan Banana, an African 'top dog', who, it is reported, has expressed his wish to have his ashes scattered on his national football team pitch so that they will always have twelve men.